Acclaim

Peter Kreeft, Boston College
Clear, compassionate, uncompromisingly Christian, and
straight from (and to) the heart. . . . Pretty close, I think, to
what Jesus would say if he were to write a book about sex
today – and probably as socially acceptable as he was.

Joan Brown Campbell
A cogent, well-reasoned approach to today's troubling questions. Some may disagree with this or that conclusion, but all
will acknowledge Arnold's sincerity and his contribution to
these debates.

William H. Willimon, Duke Divinity School
Arnold writes simply, eloquently, and faithfully. His *Sex, God,
and Marriage* is a relentless, biblical call for renewed Christian
commitment. Advocates of accommodated, acculturated
Christianity will find little comfort in these pages; struggling
disciples, however, will be much encouraged.

William A. Dyrness, Fuller Theological Seminary
Striking for its clear and penetrating presentation of simple
(and yet immensely profound) biblical truths about human
sexuality. I wish everyone could read this call to cut through
the complications of modern life by a holy and Christ-like life.

Molly Kelly, author, *Saved Sex*
I strongly recommend this book. . . . A wonderful resource for
the promotion of chastity, health, and holiness.

Paul C. Vitz, New York University
To advocate an ideal of sexual purity is perhaps the last
American taboo. . . . This book provides a wise spiritual guide
on how, and why, to lead such a life.

Richard John Neuhaus, *First Things*
Human sexuality is here drawn fully into the life of
discipleship. The result is both demanding and exhilarating,
which is what disciples of Jesus should expect.

Bob Fryling, InterVarsity Christian Fellowship
Does a wonderful job of putting sex into the larger contexts
of creation, the church, and marriage. Not everyone will agree
with all of Arnold's conclusions, but every mature believer will
benefit from the convictions reflected in this book.

Paul Brand, M.D., author, *Pain: The Gift Nobody Wants*
A clear message for those who have seen the so-called freedom
of sexual pleasure become a source of loneliness or pain. . . .
This book will help young people to hold on to purity.

Charles E. Blake, Presiding Bishop, Church of God in Christ
Arnold's bold statement on the meaning of marriage clarifies
for the sometimes confused church a concept central to
Christian teaching. In so doing Arnold provides help and
guidance that extends beyond the church to the world at large
and provides a rich resource for working with young people.
We thank God for his life, witness, and work.

Alice von Hildebrand, Hunter College
Arnold's beautiful presentation of the great virtue of purity
should be in the hands of every educator and every teenager.
It is a message that is desperately needed today, and I cannot
recommend it strongly enough.

J. I. Packer, author, *Knowing God*
A clear vision of God's ideal for marriage and family. Simple
and short, but deep, this is one of the best books available to
help us handle our sexuality in a way that honors God.

Francis Cardinal Arinze
Clear, incisive, and uplifting . . . this book should be very
helpful in living the virtue of chastity, which is God's will for
all men and women.

Sex, God & Marriage

Sex, God & Marriage

Johann Christoph Arnold

Plough Publishing House

Published by Plough Publishing House
Walden, New York
Robertsbridge, England
Elsmore, Australia
www.plough.com

Scripture quotations, unless indicated otherwise, are from New International
Version © 1973, 1978, 1984, 2011 by Biblica, Inc. Used by permission.
All rights reserved worldwide.

Front cover photograph: Corbis Images

Pope Benedict XVI's words on the cover are excerpted from a personal letter
he wrote to the author, December 1995.

To protect the privacy of individuals who contributed to this book,
several names have been changed.

Original Title: *A Plea for Purity*
Fifth Edition (softcover) ISBN 978-0-87486-650-6
20 19 18 17   3 4 5 6 7 8 9

A catalog record for this book is available from the British Library

Library of Congress Cataloging-in-Publication Data for a previous edition of
this title:

Arnold, Johann Christoph, 1940–
    Sex, God & marriage / Johann Christoph Arnold.-- 3rd ed.
    p. cm.
    Rev. ed. of: A plea for purity. 1998.
    Includes bibliographical references and index.
    ISBN-10: 0-87486-072-5 (1st ed., 1996 : alk. paper)
    ISBN-10: 0-87486-960-9 (2nd ed., 1998 : alk. paper)
    ISBN-13: 978-0-87486-941-5 (3rd ed., 2008 : alk. paper)
    1. Sex--Religious aspects--Christianity. 2. Marriage--Religious
aspects--Christianity. 3. Sex--Religious aspects--Bruderhof Communities.
4. Marriage--Religious aspects--Bruderhof Communities. 5. Bruderhof
Communities--Doctrines. I. Title: Sex, God, and marriage. II. Arnold,
Johann Christoph, 1940– Plea for purity. III. Title.
    BT708.A75 2008
    248.4'897--dc22
                                                        2008018220

Printed in the U.S.A.

*To my faithful wife, Verena, without whose help
this book would not have been possible.*

Other Titles by the Author

Be Not Afraid
Overcoming the Fear of Death

Cries from the Heart
Stories of Struggle and Hope

Escape Routes
For People Who Feel Trapped in Life's Hells

Rich in Years
Finding Peace and Purpose in a Long Life

Seeking Peace
Notes and Conversations along the Way

Their Name is Today
Reclaiming Childhood in a Hostile World

Why Children Matter

Why Forgive?

All titles available at *www.plough.com*

Contents

The author and his wife with Mother Teresa

Foreword

by Mother Teresa

IN THIS BOOK we find a message needed today in
every part of the world. To be pure, to remain pure, can
only come at a price, the price of knowing God and of
loving him enough to do his will. He will always give us
the strength we need to keep purity as something beautiful for God. Purity is the fruit of prayer. If families pray
together they will remain in unity and purity, and love
each other as God loves each one of them.

*a pure heart is a carrier
of God's love and where
there is love, there is unity
joy and Peace.
Let us pray. God bless you.
llu Teresa mc*

Introduction

EVERYWHERE TODAY, people are searching for lasting and meaningful relationships. The myth of free love continues to be taken for granted by millions, and a new generation of young men and women has accepted the belief that sexual freedom is the key to fulfillment. But as desperately as people want to believe in the sexual revolution of the last few decades, it is clear to many of them that something has gone terribly wrong. Instead of bringing freedom, "sexual liberation" has left countless wounded and isolated souls. As we face the great anguish around us, it is more important than ever for all of us, young and old, to consider the direction of our lives and ask ourselves where we are headed.

The twenty-first century heralds the loss of the clear teachings of the New Testament on marriage and the relationship of the sexes. We have turned against God and rebelled against his order of creation, and we have justified our rebellion with human arguments. We have ignored the words of Jesus and scorned the voice of the Spirit. But we have found neither freedom nor fulfillment.

As a pastor I have counseled many people over the years, both single and married. For many of them, the sexual sphere is not an area of joy but one of frustration, confusion, and even despair. People look for unity of heart and soul with one another, but they are so blinded by the notion of romantic love that their deepest longings remain obscured. They may know that sexual union in marriage is a gift from God; that it should be the most intimate and rewarding relationship a man and a woman can share. But they wonder why it has become the source of such loneliness and pain for them and for so many others.

I am no social scientist. But if the findings of recent studies have made anything clear it is this: the fallout caused by our culture's acceptance of casual sex is socially devastating. More than half of all marriages in the United States fail. Almost forty percent of America's children live in different houses than their biological fathers. Poverty, violent crime, delinquency, promiscuity, pornography, alcohol and drug abuse, mental illness, and suicide are all rooted in the breakdown of the family and the erosion of the marriage bond.

At the same time, those who save sexual activity until marriage (though their numbers are dwindling) are far less likely to have an affair or divorce, and those who commit themselves to one lifelong partner lead happier lives.[1]

While current trends point to continuing decay, there are encouraging signs that people are willing to call into question the thrills of cheap sex and the seeming ease of uncommitted love. There is an increased yearning among young people to find genuine relationships and to build secure homes, giving renewed hope that a two-parent family is still possible.

Again and again I have seen that when people are willing to surrender their lives to Jesus, they are able to find a way out of their unhappiness. Once people have the courage and humility to heed his call to repent – to turn completely around – he can bring them lasting freedom and happiness.

Jesus brings true revolution. He is the original source of love, because he is Love itself. His teaching is neither a matter of prudishness nor of permissiveness: he offers his followers an entirely different way. He brings a purity that liberates us from sin and leads to the possibility of a completely new life.

There is very little in today's culture that nurtures or protects the new life that Jesus wants to give us. People talk about the importance of meaningful relationships, of committed marriages and wholesome family life, but how many of us know what to do to make these values a concrete reality? Many of us are tempted to blame society for the influences that corrupt us. But what about us so-called Christians? How many of us are ready to stop watching television and take a hard look at our own marriages and relationships and our personal lives? How many of us actually support those around us in the daily struggle for purity? How many of us stick out our necks to confront the sin in each other's lives? How many of us are really accountable?

There is tremendous pain among those who claim to be followers of Christ: broken families, battered wives, neglected and abused children, and sinful relationships. Yet instead of an outcry, there is indifference. When will we wake up and realize that our apathy is destroying us?

More than ever, we need to come back to an understanding of the church as a living body of committed members who share life in practical deeds of love. But we must start with ourselves first and then see where we can encourage those around us. We need to know our youth well enough to be able to guide them as they seek relationships and lifetime commitments; we need to provide ongoing support for the marriages around us; we need to work for healing when our brothers or sisters stumble or fall – and accept their help when we ourselves have fallen.

Most of all, we must show the world that the unique teachings of Jesus and his apostles are the only answer to the spirit of our time. That is why I have written this book. I am neither a biblical scholar nor a professional therapist, and I am fully aware that most of what I have written is completely contrary to popular wisdom. But I do feel the urgent need to share my certainty that Jesus' call to a life of love, purity, honesty, and commitment is our only hope.

This is not only a personal book – it comes out of the life of the church community I serve, and everything in it reflects the concerns and experiences of its members. My hope is that all of us – all men and women of our time – might stop to reconsider God's purpose for sex and marriage.

Sadly, too many people today have simply given up on the possibility of a pure life. They have bought into the myth of sexual "liberation" and tried to live with its disappointments, and when their relationships fall apart, they explain away their failures. They fail to see what a tremendous gift purity is.

All the same, I believe that deep in every heart there is a yearning for unclouded relationships and for a love that lasts. It takes courage and self-discipline to really *live* a different way, but it is possible. Wherever there is a faithful church – a community of people who are committed to living in genuine and honest relationships – there is help and hope for every person and every marriage. May this book give each reader that faith.

Johann Christoph Arnold

In the Beginning

I

In the Image of God

Then God said, "Let us make mankind in our image, in our likeness, so that they may rule over the fish in the sea and the birds in the sky, over the livestock and all the wild animals, and over all the creatures that move along the ground." So God created mankind in his own image, in the image of God he created them; male and female he created them. God blessed them and said to them, "Be fruitful and increase in number; fill the earth and subdue it. Rule over the fish in the sea and the birds in the sky and over every living creature that moves on the ground."

Genesis 1:26–28

IN THE OPENING CHAPTER of the story of creation we read that God created humankind – both male and female – in his own image, and that he blessed them and commanded them to be fruitful and to care for the earth. Right from the start, God shows himself as the creator who "saw all that he had made, and it was very good." Here, right at the beginning of the Bible, God reveals his heart to us. Here we discover God's plan for our lives.

Many, if not most, modern Christians dismiss the story of creation as a myth. Others insist that only the strictest, most literal interpretation of Genesis is valid.

I simply have reverence for the word of the Bible as it stands. On the one hand, I would not think of arguing away anything in it; on the other, I believe that scientific discoveries should caution us not to take the biblical account of creation too literally. As Peter says, "With the Lord a day is like a thousand years, and a thousand years are like a day" (2 Pet. 3:8).

God's image sets us apart.

Exactly how human beings were created remains a mystery for the creator alone to unveil. Yet I am sure of one thing: no person can find meaning or purpose without God. Rather than dismiss the creation story simply because we do not understand it, we need to find its inner, true meaning and rediscover its significance for us today.

In our depraved age, reverence for God's plan as described in Genesis has been almost completely lost. We do not treasure the meaning of creation enough – the significance of both man and woman as creatures formed in the image and likeness of God. This likeness sets us apart in a special way from the rest of creation and makes each human life sacred (Gen. 9:6). To view life in any other way – for instance, to view others only in the light of their usefulness, and not as God sees them – is to disregard their worth and dignity.

What does creation "in God's image" mean? It means that we are to be a living picture of who God is. It means that we are to be coworkers who further his work of creating and nurturing life. It means that we belong to him, and that our being, our very existence, should always remain related to him and bound to his authority. The moment we separate ourselves from God we lose sight of our purpose here on earth.

In Genesis we read that we have the living spirit of God: "Then the Lord God formed a man from the dust of the ground and breathed into his nostrils the breath of life, and the man became a living being" (Gen. 2:7). In giving us his spirit, God made us responsible beings who possess the freedom to think and act, and to do so in love.

But even if we possess a living spirit, we remain only images of the creator. And when we look at creation in a God-centered, not human-centered, way we will understand our true place in his divine order of things. The person who denies that God is his origin, who denies that God is a living reality in his life, will soon be lost in a terrible emptiness. Ultimately, he will find himself trapped in the self-idolatry that brings with it self-contempt and a contempt for the worth of others.

All of us long for what is imperishable.

What would we be if God had not breathed his breath into us? Darwin's whole theory of evolution, by itself, is dangerous and futile because it is not God-centered. Something inside each of us cries out against the idea that we have been hatched by a purposeless universe. Deep within the human spirit is a thirst for what is lasting and imperishable.

Since we are made in God's image, and God is eternal, we cannot, at the end of life, merely vanish again like smoke. Our life is rooted in eternity. Christoph Blumhardt writes, "Our lives bear the mark of eternity, of the eternal God who created us in his image. He does not want us to be swallowed up in what is transitory, but calls us to what is eternal."[2]

God has set eternity in our hearts, and deep within each of us is a longing for eternity. When we deny this and live only for the present, everything that happens to us in life will remain cloaked in tormenting riddles, and we will remain deeply dissatisfied. This is especially true in the sexual area. Casual sex desecrates the soul's yearning and capacity for that which is eternal. No person, no human arrangement, can ever fill this longing of our souls.

The voice of eternity speaks most directly to our conscience. Therefore the conscience is perhaps the deepest element within us. It warns, rouses, and commands us in our God-given task (Rom. 2:14–16). And every time the soul is wounded, our conscience makes us painfully aware of it. If we listen to our conscience, it can guide us. When we are separated from God, however, our conscience will waver and go astray. This is true not only for an individual, but also for a marriage.

Already in Genesis, chapter 2, we read about the importance of marriage. When God created Adam, he said that everything he had made was good. Then he created woman to be a helpmate and partner to man, because he saw that it was not good for man to be alone. This is a deep mystery: man and woman – the masculine and the feminine – belong together as a picture of who God is, and both can be found in him. Together they become what neither would be apart and alone.

Everything created by God gives us an insight into his nature – mighty mountains, immense oceans, rivers, and great expanses of water; storms, thunder and lightning, huge icebergs; meadows, flowers, trees, and ferns. There is power, harshness, and manliness, but there is also gentleness, motherliness, and sensitivity. And just as the various forms of life in nature do not exist without each other, God's children, too, male and female, do not exist alone. They are different, but they are both made in God's image, and they need each other to fulfill their true destinies.

When God's image is defaced,
life's relationships lose purpose.

It is a tragedy that in much of today's society the differences between man and woman are blurred and distorted. The pure, natural image of God is being destroyed. There is endless talk about women's equality, but in practice women are abused and exploited more than ever before. In films, on television, in magazines, and on billboards the ideal woman (and increasingly, the ideal man) is portrayed as a mere sex object.

Generally speaking, marriages in our society are no longer regarded as sacred. Increasingly they are seen as experiments or as contracts between two people who measure everything in terms of their own interests. When marriages fail, there is the option of no-fault divorce, and after that a new attempt at marriage with a new partner. Many people no longer even bother to make promises of faithfulness; they just live together. Women who bear and raise children or stay married to the same husband are sometimes scorned. And even when their marriage is a healthy one, they are often seen as victims of oppression who need to be "rescued" from male domination.

Children are often no longer treasured. In Genesis, God commanded, "Be fruitful and increase." Today we avoid the "burden" of unwanted offspring by means of legalized abortion. Children are viewed as a bother; they are too expensive to be brought into the world, to be raised, to be given a college education. They are an economic strain on our materialistic lives. They are even too time-consuming to love.

Is it any wonder that so many in our time have lost hope? That so many have given up on the possibility of enduring love? Life has lost its value; it has become cheap; most people no longer see it as a gift from God. Advances in biomedical engineering and in fetus screening techniques enable growing numbers of couples to choose an abortion for selfish reasons. Without God, life is absurd, and there is only darkness and the deep wound of separation from him.

Despite the efforts of many dedicated individuals, the church today has failed miserably in grappling with this situation. All the more, each of us must go back to the beginning and ask ourselves once again, "Why did God create man and woman in the first place?" God created every person in his image, and he has set a specific task for every man, woman, and child on this earth, a task he expects us to fulfill. No one can disregard God's purpose for his creation or for himself without suffering deep inner need (Ps. 7:14–16).

The materialism of our time has emptied life of moral and spiritual purpose. It separates us from one another, and it hinders us from seeing the world with awe and wonder and from seeing our true task. The sickness of soul and spirit brought about by consumerism has eaten so deeply into our conscience that it is no longer able to mirror good and evil clearly. Yet there is still a deep-seated need in each of us that makes us long for what is good and right.

We will find healing only if we believe firmly that God created us and that he is the giver of life, love, and mercy. As we read in the third chapter of the Gospel of John, "God so loved the world that he gave his only son, that whoever believes in him should not perish but have eternal life. For God sent his son into the world, not to condemn the world, but that the world might be saved through him."

In God's son – in Jesus – the creator's image appears with utmost clarity and finality (Col. 1:15). As the perfect image of God, and as the only way to the Father, he brings us life and unity, joy and fulfillment. Only when our life is lived in him can we experience his truth and goodness, and only in him can we find our true destiny. This destiny is to be God's image; to rule over the earth in his spirit, which is the creative, life-giving spirit of love.

2

It Is Not Good
for Man to Be Alone

*The Lord God said, "It is not good for the man to
be alone. I will make a helper suitable for him. . . ."
So the Lord God caused the man to fall into a deep
sleep; and while he was sleeping, he took one of the
man's ribs and then closed up the place with flesh.
Then the Lord God made a woman from the rib he
had taken out of the man, and he brought her to the
man. The man said, "This is now bone of my bones
and flesh of my flesh; she shall be called 'woman,'
for she was taken out of man."*

Genesis 2:18, 21–23

THERE IS LITTLE that is so difficult for a person to
bear as loneliness. Prisoners held in solitary confinement
have told of rejoicing to see even a spider – at least it is
something alive. God created us to be communal beings.
Yet our modern world is frighteningly devoid of relationships. In many areas of life, technological progress has
resulted in the deterioration of community. Increasingly,
technology has made people seem unnecessary.

As the elderly are placed into retirement communities
or personal-care homes, as factory workers are replaced
by hi-tech robotics, as young men and women search in

vain for meaningful employment, they fall into cycles of hopelessness. Some depend on the help of therapists or psychologists, and others seek avenues of escape such as alcohol, drugs, or suicide. Cut off from God and each other, thousands of people lead lives of quiet desperation.

To live in isolation, whether outwardly or inwardly, can lead to despair. Thomas Merton writes:

> Despair is the absolute extreme of self-love. It is reached when a man deliberately turns his back on all help from anyone else in order to taste the rotten luxury of knowing himself to be lost. . . .
>
> Despair is the ultimate development of a pride so great and so stiff-necked that it selects the absolute misery of damnation rather than accept happiness from the hands of God and thereby acknowledge that he is above us and that we are not capable of fulfilling our destiny ourselves.
>
> But a man who is truly humble cannot despair, because in a humble man there is no longer any such thing as self-pity.[3]

We see here that pride is a curse that leads to death. Humility, however, leads to love. Love is the greatest gift given to humankind; it is our true calling. It is the "yes" to life, the "yes" to community. Love alone fulfills the longing of our innermost being.

God created us to live with and for others.

God has planted in each of us an instinctive longing to achieve a closer likeness to him, a longing that urges us toward love, community, and unity. In his last prayer, Jesus points out the importance of this longing: "May they all be one, as thou, Father, art in me, and I in thee, so also may they be in us, that the world may believe that thou didst send me" (John 17:20–21 NEB).

No one can truly live without love: it is God's will for every person to be the "thou" for every other. Every person is called to love and help those around him on God's behalf (Gen. 4:8–10).

God wants us to find community with one another and to help one another in love. And there is no doubt that when we meet our brother's or sister's inmost heart, we can help them, for "our" help is given by God himself. As John says, "We know that we have passed from death to life, because we love each other. Anyone who does not love remains in death" (1 John 3:14). Our lives are fulfilled only when love is kindled, proved, and brought to fruition.

Jesus tells us that the two most important commandments are to love God with our whole heart, soul, and strength, and to love our neighbor as ourselves. And these two commandments cannot be separated: love to God must always mean love to one's neighbor. We cannot find a relationship with God if we disregard others (1 John 4:19–21). Our way to God must be through our brothers and sisters, and in marriage, through our spouse.

If we are filled with God's love, we can never be lonely or withdrawn for long; we will always find someone to reach out to. God and our neighbor will always be near us. All we need to do is find them. Recently a young man in my community shared with me his newly discovered joy in reaching out to others. Sean had been living in Baltimore doing volunteer work building homes for the disadvantaged. He thought that this would be enough. However, when he came home at the end of the day he didn't know what to do:

> I found myself wasting away in front of the television. My zest for life was rapidly diminishing. Then someone told me about an evening tutoring program for inner-city children. They were desperately looking for help. So I decided to check it out. Now I help out every night. I can't believe how my whole perspective on life has changed. I never knew before how much I needed to love these children.

When we suffer from loneliness, it is often simply because our focus is on ourselves; we desire to be loved rather than to give love. Real happiness comes from giving love to others. We need to seek community of love with our neighbor again and again, and in this seeking we must each become a helper, a brother or a sister. Let us ask God to free our choked-up hearts for this love, knowing that we can find it only in the humility of the cross.

Every person can be an instrument of God's love.

In the story of the creation of Adam and Eve it is clear that man and woman were created to help, to support, to complement each other. What a joy it must have been for God to bring woman to man, and man to woman! Because we are all made in the image of God, in his likeness, we can all find each other in joy and love, whether we are married or not.

By bringing Eve to Adam, God shows all humans their true calling – to be helpers who reveal his love to the world. And by bringing us his son, Jesus, he shows us that he will never leave us lonely or without help. Jesus himself said, "I will not leave you orphaned; I will come to you." He promises us that "the man who has received my commandments and obeys them – he it is who loves me; and he who loves me will be loved by my Father; and I will love him and disclose myself to him" (John 14:18–21 NEB).

Who can understand the depth of these words and the hope they bring to our troubled world? The loneliest, most discouraged, disillusioned people may be assured that God will never forsake them. Even if they are unable to find human friendship, they will never be alone as long as they hold on to God.

God brought Adam and Eve together to heal their loneliness and to set them free from their one-sidedness, and he has the same plan for every man and woman he brings together in marriage. Yet marriage in itself cannot bring wholeness. Unless we abide in Christ, we will not bear good fruit. When we love him who alone is our support, our hope, and our life, we can be secure in knowing and loving one another. But if we isolate ourselves from Christ, nothing will go well. He alone holds everything together and gives us access to God and to others (Col. 1:17–20).

God is the source and the object of true love.

Marriage is not the highest goal of life. God's image is reflected most brightly and completely where there is love first for him and then for our brothers and sisters. In a true Christian marriage, then, the husband will lead his wife and children not to himself, but to God. In the same way, a wife will support her husband as a helper, and together they will raise their children to honor them as father and mother, and to love God as their creator.

To be a helper to another on God's behalf is not just an obligation, but a gift. How different our relationships would be if we rediscovered this! We live in a time when fear and mistrust grip us everywhere we go. Where is love, the love that builds community and the church?

There are two kinds of love. One is turned selflessly toward others and their well-being. The other is possessive and limited to the ego. Augustine says, "Love is the self of the soul, the hand of the soul. When it holds one thing, it cannot hold something else. If it is to hold what one gives it, it has to put down what it is holding."[4] God's love desires nothing. It gives and sacrifices itself, for this is its joy.

Love always has its roots in God. "We love because he first loved us" (1 John 4:19). May God grant that the power of his love grips us anew. It will lead us to others, to share our lives with them. More than that, it will lead us to the kingdom. Love is the secret of God's coming kingdom.

3

They Shall Become One Flesh

That is why a man leaves his father and mother
and is united to his wife, and they become one flesh.
Genesis 2:24

MARRIAGE IS SACRED. IN the Old Testament, the
prophets use it to describe God's relationship with his
people Israel: "I will betroth you to me forever; I will
betroth you in righteousness and justice, in love and
compassion. I will betroth you in faithfulness, and you
will acknowledge the Lord" (Hos. 2:19–20). God reveals
his love to all people in a special way in the unique bond
between husband and wife.

Marriage is more than living happily together.

In the New Testament, marriage is used as a symbol for
the unity of Christ with his church. In the Gospel of John,
Jesus is compared to a bridegroom, and in Revelation we
read that "the wedding of the Lamb has come, and his
bride has made herself ready" (Rev. 19:7).

It is not without significance that Jesus changed
water into wine at a wedding; clearly, he had great joy in
marriage. Yet it is equally clear that to Jesus, marriage is
a holy matter. He takes it so seriously that he speaks with
uncompromising sharpness against even the slightest

step toward its destruction: "Therefore what God has joined together, let no one separate" (Matt. 19:6).

We can see from Jesus' sharpness what a horror adultery is in the eyes of God. The whole Bible protests against it, from the books of the Prophets, where the idol worship of the children of Israel is called adultery (Jer. 13:25–27), to Revelation, where we read of God's wrath against the harlot. When the bond of marriage is broken, love – the unity of spirit and soul between two – is broken and smashed, and not only between the adulterer and his spouse, but between himself and God.

In our present-day culture, the institution of marriage is on the brink of disaster. It is no longer understood as an inviolable union of one man and one woman who serve one another until death parts them. Much of what is called love is nothing but selfish desire. Even in marriage many couples live together selfishly. People are deceived in thinking that fulfillment can be found without sacrifice and faithfulness, and even though they may live together, they are afraid to forgo their personal freedoms and love each other unconditionally.

Still, amid millions of floundering and ruined marriages, God's love stands eternal and cries out for constancy and devotion. There is a voice deep within each of us, however muffled, that calls us back to faithfulness. On some level, all of us yearn to be united – with free and open hearts – to somebody, to some other "thou." And if we turn to God in the trust that such unity with another is possible, we can find the fulfillment of our longing.

True fulfillment comes from giving ourselves in love to another person. Yet love does not only seek to give; it also longs to unite. If I really love another person, I will be interested in knowing what is in him and willing to be led out of my one-sidedness. In love and humility I will help him to the possibility of a full awakening, first toward God, and then toward others. True love is never possessive. It always leads to the freedom of faithfulness and purity.

In the love and unity of the church it is possible to become of one spirit with every brother and sister, and also to become of one heart and soul with them (Acts 4:32). In the faithfulness between a husband and wife, however, God's eternal faithfulness is especially manifested, for it is God who brings every true marriage bond together. In God's unfailing love we find the strength to let love flow through our lives, and to let our gifts unfold for each other – in good times and in bad.

Sexual love can give God's love visible form.

There is a difference between the love of an engaged or married couple and the love among other men and women. Nowhere is a person more dependent on another than in marriage. There is a special joy in the heart of a married person when the beloved is near; and even when separated, there is a unique bond between them. Through the intimate relationship of marriage, something takes place which may even show in a couple's faces. As von Gagern says, "Often it is only through his wife that the husband becomes truly a man; and through her husband that the wife gains true womanhood."[5]

In a true marriage, each partner seeks the fulfillment of the other. By complementing each other, the union between husband and wife is enhanced. In their love for one another, through their faithfulness to one another, and in their fruitfulness, husband and wife reflect God's image in a mysterious and wonderful way.

In the unique bond of marriage we discover the deeper meaning of becoming one flesh. Obviously to become one flesh means to become united physically and sexually, but it is far more than that! It is a symbol of a man and a woman bound and melted together, heart, body, and soul, in mutual giving and total oneness.

When husband and wife become one flesh, they are no longer two, but actually one. Their union is the fruit of more than companionship or partnership; it is the deepest intimacy. As Friedrich Nietzsche writes, it is brought about by "the resolve of two to create a unity which is more than those who created it. It is reverence for one another and for the fulfillment of such a resolve."[6]

Only in this reverence and oneness does marriage fulfill the demands of the sexual conscience. Through the will to have children, to be fruitful and to multiply, and through the togetherness that reflects the unity of God with his creation and his people, marriage gives visible form to God's outpouring love.

When God is at the center of a marriage,
full unity of heart, soul, and body is possible.

In God's order of marriage there are at least three different levels of experience. The first, most wonderful level is unity of spirit: the oneness of heart and soul in God. In this oneness we can have community not only with our spouse but with all believing persons. The second level is unity of emotion: the current of love from one heart toward another that is so strong that a person can, so to speak, hear the heartbeat of another. The third level is physical unity: the expression of oneness found when two bodies are fused in perfect union.

Too many couples today are content with the third level alone, or perhaps the second. A marriage based only on the physical and emotional is doomed to disappointment. Even though waves of emotional or physical attraction are natural, they can leave deep wounds if they are not placed under Christ. Not long ago a woman I know told me that she and her husband had only joined my congregation because they wanted to have a church wedding – not because they were interested in committing their lives to God. "My husband and I never talked about God's vision for our lives, or about what we wanted before or after our marriage," she writes. "We were not on the same wavelength." Now her husband has deserted her and their five children. It has become painfully clear to her that because their commitment to each other was not grounded in Christ, she and her husband lacked a solid, lasting foundation for their marriage.

If a marriage is to be truly healthy, it must be founded in the order of God – on unity of spirit, heart, and soul. Most people today, including those of us who claim to be Christians, have no idea how much God has prepared for those who truly love and honor him. When we embrace God's design for our relationships, we will experience God's blessings. The experiences of the heart that God can give in a true engagement or marriage are greater than we can imagine. Too many of us live only in the world of the senses – of sleeping, eating, and drinking – and never take time to really turn to what is much more vital: our inner life. This is also true in so many marriages today. Sex is the focal point, and often unity of heart is not even sought or mentioned. Is it any wonder that so few couples remain faithful to each other for life?

Anyone who has lived near the ocean knows something of nature's power in the pull of high and low tides. In marriage, as in friendship, there are high and low tides. When a relationship is at low ebb, it is all too easy for us to lose patience, to distance ourselves from our partner, and even to abandon efforts toward a renewal of love. When God is at the center, we can turn to him and find faith and strength even at our lowest ebb.

The more we reflect the image of God in which we are created, the more strongly will we sense that God must remain our center, and that his commandments are fitting for us. We will sense that his commandments are not laid on us as alien laws and commands. Rather, we will see that they are in keeping with our true nature as beings created in his image. But the more we betray and desecrate God's image within us, the more his rulership will appear to us as something foreign, a moral compulsion that crushes us.

To be fruitful for each other, by complementing each other in love, and to be fruitful with each other in bearing children – it is these purposes that make marriage blessed and holy, and a joy in heaven. Even so, in the story of the creation, along with God's command to "be fruitful" comes a blessing: his gift of woman as a partner to the first man. In giving man and woman this gift, it is as if God is saying, "My image lives in you." Whenever we approach marriage, we must consider this with great reverence. In every person and in every marriage lives the potential for a genuine expression of the image of God.[7]

4

The First Sin

*Now the serpent was more crafty than any of the
wild animals the Lord God had made. He said to
the woman, "Did God really say, 'You must not
eat from any tree in the garden'?"... "You will not
certainly die," the serpent said to the woman. "For
God knows that when you eat from it your eyes will
be opened, and you will be like God, knowing good
and evil."*

Genesis 3:1, 4–5

WHEN GOD CREATED THE WORLD, everything he
made was good. The earth was truly his kingdom, and
life was ruled by the spirit of peace. Everything, including
man and woman, dwelled together in unity and harmony
and took delight in one another and in all that God had
made. With trembling reverence and wonder Adam and
Eve stood before the life-filled tree in the Garden of
Eden. But then the serpent misled Adam and Eve. Immediately, evil came into God's creation and tried to destroy
it completely.

Eve was tempted by the serpent with one simple question: "Did God really say that?" and with one simple
promise: "Surely you will not die!" It is important that we
understand what this means. Satan, the seducer, tempted
Eve with words of God, just as later he tempted Jesus with
words of God.

Pride separates us from God and from each other.
What else was it, if not pride, when Eve looked at the tree
and lusted for its fruit, wanting to make herself like God?
Was she not testing God to see whether he would really
keep his word? The serpent put doubt into her heart, and
Eve listened to him with great curiosity. That in itself
was a betrayal of God, and it gives us an insight into how
Satan still works today.

Satan still wants to separate us from God and from one
another. And if we are not watchful, he can do it simply
by asking a seemingly innocent question that sows seeds
of mistrust and division in our hearts. Satan disguises
himself as an angel of light (2 Cor. 11:14), but actually he
is the slanderer, the twister of truth, the father of lies,
the murderer from the beginning; he tries to throw us
into disorder and confusion and doubt – and very often
he succeeds.

In the Gospel of Matthew we read that shortly after
Jesus' baptism, when he withdrew into the wilderness,
Satan tried to tempt him. Knowing that Jesus was physically weak after fasting for forty days, Satan approached
Jesus with a face of compassion and showed false reverence by suggesting that all the kingdoms of the world
should belong to him.

Yet already in that first temptation, Jesus recognized
Satan as the tempter, and the twister of truth. He trusted
in God unconditionally and did not consider listening
to Satan for even a moment, but rather went the way of
trust, obedience, and dependence on God. Satan could
not come close to his heart.

It was not just the forbidden fruit that enticed Adam
and Eve, but pride and the self-seeking desire to be like

God. Because they lacked trust, obedience, and dependence, they cut themselves off from God. In the end, because they no longer honored him, they made idols of each other.

The greatest curse on our human destiny is the attempt to become like God. Bonhoeffer says, "In following Satan's temptations to be like God yet independent of him, man has become a god against God."[8] The result is a deep sickness in the human spirit. The image of God is now a stolen image, and twisted by idolatry and rebellion against him, it brings great darkness and need (Rom. 1:23–32).

False love hinders the joy of total giving.

Adam and Eve both sinned against God's love, against his good plan. They were deceived by a false love: human desire. How many things happen today that go by the name of love and are nothing but destruction and soul-murder!

> True love wants the person of God to shine through the beloved: God remains the value by which love is measured and the final goal of love's striving. But man, in a false love to the beloved, turns away from the highest good and thereby makes it impossible for God to shine through the beloved.[9]

All this should be a serious warning to us, whether we are married or hoping to be married. God alone must be first in our lives, not our spouse, not our children. In our own marriage, my wife and I learned that when God did not have the first and foremost place in our relationship, and when we did not turn to him for guidance even in small matters, we soon lost our closeness to each other. This affected our children too (even if they were not conscious of it), by making them disobedient and quarrelsome. I have seen the same occur in many families: when a couple drifts apart, their children act out their insecurities. In our case, as with many other couples, once my wife and I turned back to God and sought to rebuild our relationship, our children responded.

When we idolize our spouse or our children, our love becomes false. We cannot speak freely about our shortcomings or those of our family. Like Adam, we no longer truly love God or see his countenance; we see only our spouse's or our children's. Rather than address issues head-on, we gloss things over. In this way, we eventually lose touch with God and with each other. Worse, we open the door to evil, especially in the sexual area, and to inner deadness and isolation. Adam and Eve lost their innocence because they lost their unity with God. And through the terrible emptiness that followed, man blamed woman and sought to dominate, and woman, resentful of man, blamed Satan. All unity was destroyed, and man and woman became rivals and were no longer one (Gen. 3:7–19).

When our marriages are separated from God, rivalry soon takes root and selfishness and mistrust consume us. In competing with our spouse to rule the roost, we strive to create our own little paradise on our own terms, and we soon sink into emptiness and deep discontent. Our inner bond is destroyed and we remain bound to one another only through infatuation. We continually blame each other and seek our own advantage and independence. The joy of total giving is gone and only the curse of half-heartedness is left.

The enemy of life in God is an independent and covetous will. As my grandfather Eberhard Arnold writes, this will is "the commercial spirit of mammon, the legal spirit of property-based relationships, the detachment of sexual desire from the soul and from unity and community of spirit. . . . All this is death; it is no longer connected with life."[10]

Anything that stands in opposition to life and love is evil, and we should never underestimate the power of evil. Sin always leads to separation, and the wages of sin is always death (Rom. 6:23). Sinful pride bears its bitter fruit in estrangement – separation from God, from our true selves, from others, and from the earth. Satan and sin shatter the most fundamental relationships we have.

From ancient times on, Christians have pictured Satan as a creature with hooves and horns. Such a notion has no biblical basis. Satan and his demons surround the earth like an atmosphere, a force of evil that seeks to separate and divide us (Eph. 2:1–2; 6:12). His sole aim is to blind humans with self-interest and egoism: "You will be like God." And instead of going the way of simple obedience, we allow ourselves to be tempted and give in.

*Like Adam and Eve, all of us are divided
and estranged by our sin.*

Adam and Eve's first sin symbolizes the fall of each one of us. We cannot ignore the fact that the original image of God in us has been terribly distorted. Instead of being content to reflect the image of God, we strive for equality with God. We have turned the highest qualities within us against God's will. In our worldly "freedom" we are no longer even concerned about God or his image. We are estranged from him and moved only by the affairs of the world. We are at odds with ourselves and one another, trapped by the guilt of our own dividedness.

Cut off from God in this way, we place ourselves at the center of the universe and try to find peace in possessions and pleasure. But these idols only leave us troubled with anxiety and anguish. Then arises the first mistrustful question, "Why?" and the second, "Is God really there?" We begin to doubt the guidance of the Spirit, and we ask, "Why do I have it so hard? Why me?"

Such questions eat away at our trust, not only in God but in each other, and when we ask them we are never far from sinning. Simple faith takes the hand that God is offering and goes the way he leads. Even if the way leads through darkness or suffering, through hard places, over rocks and deserts, trust will help us to follow. If we take God's hand, nothing can harm us. But as soon as we let go of God and question him, we will begin to despair. That is always the challenge: to hold on to God.

Jesus had to endure every human suffering; he was spared nothing – not hunger, thirst, loneliness, temptation, nor torment. But he did not attempt to escape from his misery. He is near to us, and he is always ready to help us, to give us the strength to overcome (Heb. 2:14–18). Even the most satanic temptations, the most terrible hours of darkness, are overcome by these words of Jesus: "Worship the Lord your God, and serve him only" (Matt. 4:10). This is the secret. Here Satan loses all power over us, and the first sin no longer binds.

5

Restoring the Image of God

The Lord is the Spirit, and where the Spirit of the Lord is, there is freedom. And we all, who with unveiled faces contemplate the Lord's glory, are being transformed into his image with ever-increasing glory, which comes from the Lord, who is the Spirit.... Therefore, if anyone is in Christ, the new creation has come: The old has gone, the new is here!

2 Corinthians 3:17–18; 5:17

MORE IMPORTANT than any human relationship is our relationship to God. All other relationships are merely symbols of it. First and foremost, we bear God's image and we need to find reverence for that fact again and again.

The greatest hope for every person, and for every relationship or marriage, is to recognize that even though we have distorted this image and fallen away from God, a faint reflection still remains in us. Despite our corruption, God does not want us to lose our destiny as creatures made in his image. Therefore he sent his son Jesus, the second Adam, to break into our hearts (Rom. 5:17–19). Through Jesus the image of God can be restored in every man and woman, and to every relationship.

Jesus opens the way to God and to each other.

Jesus is God's reconciler: he has come to reconcile us to God and to others and to heal the inner discord in our lives (Eph. 2:11–19). When we become discouraged or downcast, then more than ever we must seek him. Everyone who seeks will find God. This is a promise. Jeremiah says, "You will seek me and find me when you seek me with all your heart" (Jer. 29:13). And there are the wonderful words in the gospels: "Everyone who asks receives; the one who seeks finds; and to the one who knocks, the door will be opened" (Luke 11:10). These words are true today, and if we take them seriously, God will become living in our hearts.

The way to God is open for everyone. No human being is excluded from this gift, because Jesus came as a human being and lived among us. God sent him to restore his image in us. Through him we have access to the Father. But this can only happen when the experience of Pentecost – of personal repentance, conversion, and faith – becomes a burning reality for us.

The miracle of Pentecost, in which the Holy Spirit descended to earth in power and love, can happen anywhere in the world at any time. It can happen wherever people cry out, "Brothers, sisters, what shall we do?" and wherever they are ready to hear the age-old answer of Peter, "Repent and be baptized, every one of you, in the name of Jesus Christ for the forgiveness of your sins. . . . Save yourselves from this corrupt generation" (Acts 2:37–40).

Freedom comes through surrender,
not human strength.

We can find forgiveness and salvation only at the cross. At the cross we undergo death – a dying to self-will. This death liberates us from everything that has prevented fellowship with God and with others and renews our relationship with them. In giving up the sin and evil which has enslaved us, we find freedom in Jesus. We can never redeem ourselves or better ourselves by our own strength. All we can do is surrender ourselves completely to Jesus and his love, so that our lives no longer belong to us but to him.

My father, J. Heinrich Arnold, writes:

> If we want to be healed of the wounds made by Satan's tricks and arrows . . . we must have the same absolute trust in Jesus as he had in God. Ultimately, all we have is our sin. But we must lay our sin before him in trust. Then he will give us forgiveness, cleansing, and peace of heart; and these lead to a love that cannot be described.[11]

What does it mean to "lay our sin before him in trust?" Freedom and the possibility for reconciliation begin whenever we confess the accusations of our conscience. Sin lives in darkness and wants to remain there. But when, as the following story of an acquaintance, Darlene, shows, we bring to light the sins that burden us – when we admit them without reserve – we can be cleansed and freed:

> By the ninth grade, I had picked out my "future husband." I spent many secret hours writing to him in my diary, dreaming about him, and watching his house

in the hope of seeing him through a window. Several years later he married someone else, and my fantasy world fell apart.

Through my high school years I tried to be part of the "in" crowd, always conscious of what I said, did, and wore. But by the time I graduated, I had flirted with countless boys, and though I felt guilty about this because of my upbringing, I simply chose to ignore it. I squashed my protesting conscience and convinced myself that I could handle any situation.

After high school I traveled to Israel, intending to spend a year at a kibbutz. At first I was shocked by the constant partying and the preoccupation with sex among the teens there, but soon I was hanging out in guys' rooms and going to drinking parties and discos like everyone else. I told myself I could withdraw from any situation at any time, but within weeks I had let myself be sucked into a relationship with a boy who said he truly loved me. I wanted so much to believe him that I fell for him, even though I knew he was the Don Juan of the kibbutz. I felt more and more guilty; I could see I was doing exactly what I had claimed I was strong enough to resist. I panicked when I saw him a few nights later with another girl.

I returned home and, during the next two years, thought I had overcome my problem. But I had not. I fell again.

A man promised me a wonderful future, and he told me constantly how much he loved me and how beautiful I was. I wanted desperately to believe in him. Soon it was hand-holding, hugging, kissing, touching – one thing led to the next. As he wanted more and more from me, I completely blocked out all feelings of terrible guilt and horror. When he asked for sex, I gave in. I chose to fall deeper into sin rather than face up to the absolute mess I was in. I wanted to run away from home and live with him, and I promised him my love and loyalty – even when he threatened to kill me if I told anyone about our relationship. The next day he disappeared, and I never saw him again.

Plagued by depression, I considered suicide. My head and stomach ached incessantly. I felt I was going insane. I was obsessed with sex; I didn't see how I could go on without a man to "love" me. I went for one boy after another; two of them were even engaged to other girls. I grew desperate and wept secretly for hours. Through it all, though I felt like a prostitute, I tried to show my family and friends a happy and confident image. . . .

My double life could not last forever, and eventually I was caught in a lie. I realized then that God was giving me another chance. I might never again have such an opportunity to break out of my sin. Giving in, I turned to my parents and confessed everything. The devil was not quick to let me go, tormenting me in my sleep, but the depth of God's love became very real to me in the following weeks and months. There were constant prayers and love from my family and church, who never lost hope for me. I believe prayer drove away many evil spirits that often seemed to hover around me, especially in those first weeks.

After months of hard-fought struggle, my bondage to evil was finally severed. Then came the unforgettable moment when the forgiveness of all my sins was spoken out by my pastor, in God's stead. The power and joy of that moment knew no bounds.

When we are burdened by sin, it is a tremendous gift to find someone to talk to about it. Pouring out one's heart to another person is like opening a sluice gate in a dam – the water runs out, and the pressure disappears. If confession is honest and heartfelt, it can bring a deep feeling of relief, because it is the first step on the road to forgiveness. But ultimately we have to stand before God. We cannot run away or hide from him, as Adam and Eve tried to do when they disobeyed him. If we are willing to stand before him in the light of his son Jesus, he will burn away all our guilt.

Just as God gave the first man and woman peace and joy in the Garden of Eden, he gives every believer the task of working toward the new creation of his peaceable kingdom. To carry out this task, we must joyfully accept the rule of God in our lives and be willing to go the entire way of Jesus – to start at the stable in Bethlehem and end at the cross on Golgotha. It is a very lowly, humble walk. But it is the only way that leads to complete light and hope.

Jesus alone can forgive and remove our sins, because he alone is free from all stain. He can stir our consciences and set them free from impurity, bitterness, and discord (Heb. 9:14). If we accept the stirrings of our conscience, take responsibility for the choices we have made, and embrace God's judgment and mercy, it does not matter how far we have strayed or how corrupt we have been. In Christ, the conscience that used to be our enemy becomes our friend.

Forgiveness has power to transform our lives.

The forgiveness Jesus offers is so powerful that it will change our lives completely. Everything that makes us fearful or isolated, everything impure and deceitful, everything that prevents us from showing and receiving love, will yield if we give ourselves to him. What is up will come down, and what is down will come up. This change will start in the innermost heart of our being, and then our outward life, including all our relationships, will also be transformed.

Whether or not a person has experienced such redemption shows up most plainly when he or she faces death. Those who have been at the bedside of a dying person will know how absolute, how final in its significance, is each person's inner relationship with God. They know that in the end, when the last breaths are drawn, this bond is the only thing that counts.

It is the life-task of every person to prepare to meet God. Jesus tells us how to do this when he says, "Whatever you do for the least of them you do for me." He also says, "Blessed are the poor in spirit, for theirs is the kingdom of God." I have personally experienced at deathbeds that if a person has lived for others, as Jesus did, then God is very close to him in the last hour. I have also experienced at the hour of death the torment of those who have lived selfish and sinful lives and refuse to repent.

All of us, whether married or single, need to grasp more deeply the eternally healing words of Jesus: "Surely I am with you always, to the very end of the age" (Matt. 28:20). In Jesus there is life, love, and light. In him our lives and our relationships can be purified from all that burdens us and opposes love, and God's image in us can be restored.

6

Sexuality and
the Sensuous Sphere

*For everything God created is good, and nothing
is to be rejected if it is received with thanksgiving,
because it is consecrated by the word of God and
prayer.*

         1 Timothy 4:4–5

THE BIBLE SPEAKS of the heart as the center of a
person's inner life. In the heart, decisions are made and
the direction is set as to what kind of person we become
(Jer. 17:10). But God also created us as sensuous beings.
To the sensuous belongs everything that we perceive
with our senses, including sexual attraction. The scent
of a flower, the warmth of the sun, or a baby's first smile
brings us joy. God has given us a great gift in our senses,
and if we use them to praise and honor him, they can
bring us great happiness.

Yet just as the area of sensuous experience can bring
us close to God, it can also mislead us and even plunge us
into demonic darkness. All too often we tend toward the
superficial and miss the might and power of what God
could otherwise give us. In grasping at what we experience with our senses, we forget about God and miss the
possibility of experiencing the full depth of his will.

Lasting joy is found not in our senses, but in God.

To despise the living senses is to reject God and his handiwork (1 Tim. 4:1–3). The Holy Spirit does not want us to ignore the body or its emotional powers. But we should not forget that Satan seeks to undermine every good thing; he is a twister of the truth and is always waiting to deceive us, especially in this area.

Admittedly, the soul is drawn to God through the spirit, but it is always joined to the physical through the body. Our physical being is not the real enemy of the spirit, and it must never be rejected. The real enemy is Satan, who continually tries to attack the human soul and sever it from God. God's will is that every part of life – spirit, soul, and body – be brought under his control for his service (1 Cor. 10:31).

In and of itself there is nothing wrong with the sphere of the senses. After all, everything we do, whether waking or sleeping, involves a sensory experience at some level. But because we are not mere animals, because we are made in the image of God, far more is expected of us.

When two people fall in love, the joy they have at first is usually on a sensuous level: they look into each other's eyes, they hear one another speak, they rejoice in the touch of the other's hand, or even in the warmth of the other's closeness. Of course, the experience goes far deeper than seeing, hearing, or feeling, but it still begins as an experience of the senses.

Yet human love can never remain at this level – it must go much deeper than that. When the sensuous becomes an end in itself, everything seems fleeting and temporary, and we feel compelled to seek our satisfaction in

Sexuality and the Sensuous Sphere

experiences of greater and greater intensity (Eph. 4:17–19). Spending our energies on the intoxication of our senses, we soon exhaust and ruin our ability to experience life's vital power. And we also lose the capacity for any deep inner experiences. An acquaintance who has been married for over thirty years told me:

> When my wife and I first married, I always wanted her to dress smart and sexy. It was the heyday of the mini-skirt, and I thought she looked great in one. I did not recognize the damage this attitude did to her, to other men, and to myself. I was actually encouraging the lustful glance that Jesus so clearly denounces. Only later, when my wife and I realized this, did we find freedom from an unhealthy emphasis on each other's physical appearance and the way forward to a more genuine relationship.

Unless we submit ourselves (including our senses) in reverence to God, we will be unable to experience the things of this world to their fullest. Time and again I have seen how people who focus on gratifying their senses wind up leading shallow, aimless lives. When our senses rule our lives, we become frustrated and confused. But in God we can experience the eternal in the sensuous. In him we can satisfy our heart's deepest longings for what is genuine and lasting.

> *When we surrender our sexuality to God,*
> *it becomes a gift.*

As a gift from God, sensuality is a mystery; without God, its mystery is lost and it is desecrated. This is especially true for the whole area of sex. The sexual life has a deep intimacy all its own, which each of us instinctively hides from others. Sex is each person's secret, something that affects and expresses one's innermost being. Every disclosure in this area opens up something intimate and personal and lets another person into one's secret. Therefore the sexual sphere – even though it is one of God's greatest gifts – is also the sphere of shame. We should feel ashamed to unveil our secret before others. There is a reason for this: just as Adam and Eve were ashamed of their nakedness before God because they knew that they had sinned, all of us know that we are sinful by nature. This recognition is not an unhealthy mental disorder, as many psychologists claim. It is the instinctive response to protect that which is holy and given by God, and it should lead every person to repentance.

Sexual union is meant to be the expression and fulfillment of an enduring and unbreakable bond of love. It represents the supreme surrender to another human being because it involves the mutual revelation of each partner's most intimate secret. To engage in sexual activity of any kind without being united in the bond of marriage, therefore, is a desecration. The widespread practice of premarital sexual "experimentation," even with a partner one intends to marry, is no less terrible, and it can severely damage a future marriage. The veil of intimacy between a man and woman must not be lifted without the blessing of God and the church in marriage (Heb. 13:4).

Even within a marriage, the whole sphere of sexual intimacy must be placed under Christ if it is to bear good fruit. The contrast between a marriage where Christ is in the center and one where the flesh is the focal point is best described by the Apostle Paul in his letter to the Galatians:

> The acts of the sinful nature are obvious: sexual immorality, impurity, and debauchery; idolatry and witchcraft; hatred, discord, jealousy, fits of rage, selfish ambition, dissension, factions, and envy; drunkenness, orgies, and the like. I warn you, as I did before, that those who live like this will not inherit the kingdom of God. But the fruit of the Spirit is love, joy, peace, patience, kindness, goodness, faithfulness, gentleness, and self-control. Against such things there is no law. Those who belong to Christ Jesus have crucified the sinful nature with its passions and desires (Gal. 5:19–24).

People who see sexual lust in the same way as they see gluttony do not understand the significance of the sexual sphere. When we give in to the temptations of lust or sexual impurity, we are defiled in quite a different way than by gluttony, even though that, too, is condemned in the Bible. Lust and impurity wound us in our innermost heart and being. They attack the soul at its core. Whenever we fall into sexual impurity, we fall prey to demonic forces, and our whole being is corrupted. Then only through deep repentance and renewal can we be freed.

The opposite of impurity is not legalism.

The opposite of sexual impurity and sensuality, however, is not prudery, moralism, or false piety. How seriously Jesus warns us against this! (Matt. 23:25–28). In everything we experience with our senses, our joy must be genuine and free. Pascal says, "The passions are most alive in those who want to renounce them." When sensuality is repressed by moral compulsion rather than disciplined from within, it will only find new channels of untruthfulness and perversity (Col. 2:21–23).

In our corrupt and shameless time, it is harder and harder to raise children with a deep sense of reverence for God and all that he has created. All the more, we must strive to bring up our children in such a way that whether or not they marry as adults, they become men and women committed to a life of purity.

We must be watchful that neither we nor our children talk irreverently about sexual matters. Yet at the same time we cannot avoid the issue. Rather, we need to bring to our children a spirit of reverence. We must teach them the significance and holiness of sex in God's order, and impress on them the importance of keeping their bodies and minds pure and undefiled for the single purpose of marriage. They must learn to feel, as we do, that sex finds its deepest fulfillment, and therefore gives greatest pleasure, only in a pure and godly marriage.

God has joy when a newly married couple experiences full uniting: first in spirit, then from heart to heart and soul to soul, and then in body. When husband and wife lift the veil of sex in reverence before him, in relationship with him, and in the unity given by him, their union honors God. Every couple should strive for this reverence, for the pure in heart shall see God (Matt. 5:8).

7

The Pure in Heart

Blessed are the pure in heart, for they shall see God.

Therefore, since we have these promises, dear friends, let us purify ourselves from everything that contaminates body and spirit, perfecting holiness out of reverence for God.

Matthew 5:8; 2 Corinthians 7:1

SØREN KIERKEGAARD says that purity of heart is to will one thing. That one thing is God and his will. Apart from God, our hearts remain hopelessly divided. What is impurity, then? Impurity is separation from God. In the sexual sphere it is the misuse of sex, which occurs whenever sex is used in any way that is forbidden by him.

Impurity never pollutes us from without. It cannot be outwardly wiped away at will. Originating in our imagination, it breaks out from inside us like an infected sore (Matt. 15:16–20). An impure heart is never satisfied, never whole: it always wants to steal something for itself, and even then lusts for still more. Impurity stains the soul, corrupts the conscience, destroys the coherence of life, and eventually leads to spiritual death.

An impure heart is neither satisfied nor free.

Whenever we allow our soul to be touched by impurity, we open it to a demonic force that has power to gain control over every sphere of our life, not only the sexual. Impurity can take the form of idolatrous passion for professional sports; it can be the ambitious craving for prestige or power over other people. If we are ruled by anything but Christ, we are living in impurity.

Impurity in the sexual sphere often consists in using another person, even when there is consent, solely in order to satisfy desire. It is there wherever people enter into situations of sexual intimacy with no intention of forming a lasting bond.

One of the starkest forms of impurity occurs when a person pays money for sex. A person who does this "becomes one with the prostitute," as the Apostle Paul says, because he is using the body of another human being simply as a thing, a means of self-gratification. In doing this he commits a crime against the other person, but also against himself (1 Cor. 6:15–20). Even in marriage, sex for its own sake is sex separated from God. As Dietrich von Hildebrand writes, it possesses a poisonous sweetness that paralyzes and destroys.

It would be a grave mistake, however, to imagine that the opposite of impurity is the absence of sexual feeling. In fact, the lack of sexual awareness is not necessarily even fertile ground for purity. A person who has no sensitivity to sex is in actual fact an incomplete person: he or she lacks something not only in natural disposition, but in that which gives color to his or her whole being.

People who seek to live a pure life do not despise sex. They are simply free from prudish fear and hypocritical shows of disgust. But they never lose reverence for the mystery of sex, and they will keep a respectful distance from it until they are called by God to enter its territory through marriage.

For unmarried Christians, suppression of sexual feelings or simply avoiding the opposite sex is not the answer; only when they are surrendered completely to Christ will purity be found. In marriage, two people entrust the special holiness of the sexual area to each other. Yet in the deepest sense it is not they who give this gift to each other, but God, who created us all as sexual beings. Thus, whenever we give in to temptation – even if only in our thoughts – we are sinning against God, who created our sexuality for his purpose.

God wants to give inner harmony and decisive clarity to every heart. In this lies purity (James 4:8). As my grandfather, Eberhard Arnold, writes:

> If the heart is not clear and undivided – "single," as Jesus put it – then it is weak, flabby, and indolent, incapable of accepting God's will, of making important decisions, or of taking strong action. That is the reason why Jesus attached the greatest significance to singleness of heart, simplicity, unity, solidarity, and decisiveness. Purity of heart is nothing else than absolute integrity, which can overcome desires that enervate and divide. Determined single-heartedness is what the heart needs in order to be receptive, truthful and upright, confident and brave, firm and strong.[12]

The key to purity is humility.

In the Beatitudes Jesus blesses the pure and the meek; he says that they shall inherit the earth and see God. Purity and meekness belong together, because they both arise from complete surrender to God. In fact, they depend on it. But purity and meekness are not inborn; they must be struggled for again and again. There are few things more wonderful a Christian can strive for.

The struggle against sexual impurity is not just a problem for young adults. For many people, it does not lessen as they grow older and more mature, but remains a serious struggle for life. Certainly a desire to live a pure life is good and necessary, yet it remains impossible for anyone to simply "resolve" never to give in to temptation again. Only through the experience of forgiveness can the gift of purity be given. And even then, our battle against temptations will continue. Still, we can take courage. No matter how often or how sorely we are tempted, Jesus will plead to God on our behalf if we ask him. In him we have the promise that we can find victory over every temptation (1 Cor. 10:13).

Yet only the humble can experience God's infinite goodness. The proud never can. Proud people open their hearts to all sorts of evil: impurity, lying, stealing, and the spirit of murder. Where there is one of these sins, the others will not be far behind. People who strive for purity in their own strength will always be stumbling. Seemingly self-confident, they fall into darkness and sin because they think they can handle their problems on their own.

Each of us faces temptations in the sexual area, and our only hope in overcoming them lies in our willingness to confess our struggle to someone we trust. When we do this, we discover that we are by no means unique.

Frank, a young man who has shared with me about his struggle for purity, writes:

Even as a small child, I considered myself to be a special and "spiritual" person. Once I established this image, I found it extremely difficult to share my problems with my parents or with anyone else. As I grew up, all my energy went into being a "good" boy. I would watch people I thought were "cool," and I would try to imitate them. This self-obsession continued during my college years. I chose to follow the crowd and drift along wherever the stream of college life took me.

As I grew older, I saw my peers maturing into functional adults. Scared that I was being left behind, I refined my efforts to hide my deep insecurity, a problem that by now amounted to a mental disorder. Rather than look for suave role models, I turned to men who seemed to be spiritually gifted and tried to copy them.

As the years went by, my fear that something might be chronically wrong with my life increased. Because of my pride, I was tormented and plagued by mistrust, doubts, and hatred. At the same time I led a secret life of sexual impurity. But I suppressed all this and lived in constant fear of being found out.

Too often I have watched people who could have been helped early on lose hope and slide further into sexual sin. Like an avalanche, their problems mount. Some even fall into a life of crime, drugs, and alcohol abuse simply because they see no way out. Often all such a person needs is a friend or pastor to point him toward God and encourage him to work for the purity he actually craves. (Frank eventually confronted his desperate need and asked for help.) A person's intense self-absorption, which is often camouflaged pride, shields him from the great promise that every temptation can be overcome – if only he is willing to admit his failings and turn away from himself.

Humble people, on the other hand, live in God's strength. They may fall, but God will always lift them up and rescue them from a downward spiral.

Of course, not only our struggles but everything in our lives should be placed under Jesus. Jesus overcomes the desires that tear us apart and dissipate our strength. The more firmly we are gripped by his Spirit, the nearer we will come to finding our true character.

Who is pure in heart?

In the Sermon on the Mount we can see how seriously Jesus takes the daily fight for purity. He says that if we look at another person with a lustful glance, we have already committed adultery in our hearts (Matt. 5:27–30). The fact that Jesus warns so sharply against lustful thoughts – let alone lustful actions – should show us how important a decisive attitude of heart is in this fight.

Bonhoeffer writes, "Who is pure in heart? Only those who have surrendered their hearts completely to Jesus that he alone may remain in them; only those whose hearts are undefiled by their own evil – and by their own virtue as well."[13]

Pure men and women are able to discern both the good and the evil in the sexual sphere. They are awake to its intrinsic qualities and fully aware of its goodness and beauty as a gift from God. But they are also keenly aware that even the slightest misuse of this gift opens the door to evil spirits, and they know they cannot free themselves from these spirits in their own strength. That is why they avoid every situation, including images, that defiles the soul, and abhor the thought of leading others into sin.

It is of vital importance that in our fight for purity we reject everything that belongs to the domain of sexual immorality, including greed, vanity, and every other form of self-indulgence. Our attitude cannot be one of "partial" fascination with lust – only one of complete rejection. If our hearts are pure, we will react instinctively against anything that threatens to cloud this attitude.

Here the church community has a great responsibility to fight daily for an atmosphere of purity among all of its members (Eph. 5:3–4). Accountability and mutual support are paramount. But the fight for purity must also go hand in hand with the fight for justice and the common good, because there is no true purity of heart without a feeling for the need and suffering of others (James 1:26–27). Purity is not just related to the sexual area; to know that a neighbor is hungry and to go to bed without giving him food is to defile one's heart. That is why the early Christians pooled everything they possessed – their food and drink, their goods, their strength, even their intellectual and creative activity – and gave it up to God in service to others. Because they were of one heart and soul and held all things in common, they could battle evil in all its forms as one united fellowship.

Marriage is no guarantee of purity.

It is an illusion to think that the struggle for purity comes to an end as soon as one is married. Marriage can even be a trap. Many single people think that all their problems will be solved the minute they are married, but the fact is that many of their problems will only begin then.

Certainly, the union between husband and wife is a great grace. It can have a redeeming effect, especially in the sense of softening one's ego. But the redemptive effect of marriage in itself can never solve the need of a burdened conscience. Full redemption can be found only in Jesus.

A marriage certificate is no guarantee of purity. Whenever a living relationship with God is missing, sex quickly loses its true depth and dignity and becomes an end in itself. Even in marriage, superficiality in the sexual sphere spells ruin because it erodes the preciousness of the bond between man and woman.

It is tragic how so many today, even among Christians, use the marriage certificate as a license for satisfying every desire. A middle-aged couple I once met shared with me that, in the privacy of their own bedroom, they periodically watched pornographic videos to help "keep their love life alive." They saw nothing wrong with this. "Doesn't God want a couple to enjoy each other?" was their rationale. Little could they see how twisted and cheap their love life had become. Their attempts to substitute their lives with those of others only served to fuel their dissatisfaction with each other.

Nothing should reveal the need of God's special sanction more plainly than marriage. Therefore, whenever a man and woman unite, they should have the attitude Moses had when he came upon the burning bush: "Here is holy ground!" (Exod. 3:5). Their attitude must always be one of reverence for their creator and for the mystery of marriage.

As the union of a husband and wife under God, sex fulfills its divinely ordained purpose in a profound way: it is tender, peaceful, and mysterious. Far from being an animal-like act, it creates and expresses a unique bond of deep, self-giving love.

When a couple experiences the sexual sphere in this way, they will feel that their union cannot be meant only for procreation. At the same time, they must always be mindful that through their uniting a new life may come into being. If they are truly reverent, they will feel such awe for the holiness of this fact that their coming together will become like a prayer to God.

Without Christ, a man or woman who has lived a life of impurity cannot grasp the mysterious depths of the sexual sphere. But in Christ there can occur remarkable healing. "For we know that when he appears, we shall be like him, for we shall see him as he is. Everyone who has this hope in him purifies himself, just as he is pure" (1 John 3:3).

What God
Has Joined Together

8

Marriage in the Holy Spirit

*I urge you to live a life worthy of the calling you
have received. Be completely humble and gentle;
be patient, bearing with one another in love. Make
every effort to keep the unity of the Spirit through
the bond of peace.*

Ephesians 4:1–3

EVERY MARRIAGE goes through tests and crises, but
these can bring about an increase in love, and every new
couple should remember this. True love provides the
strength needed to meet every test. It means deeds, acts
of serving one another in humble, mutual submission.
True love is born of the Holy Spirit.

Often we overlook the depth of this truth. We tend
either to dismiss true love as some sort of flimsy fairy
tale or to focus so much energy on finding it that we miss
it entirely. But the true love that stems from the Holy
Spirit is not brought about by human effort. A married
couple who experiences its blessings will notice their love
increasing with each passing year, regardless of the trials
they may encounter. Decades into their marriage, they
will still find joy in making each other happy. As Jean, an
acquaintance who has been married for over forty years,
writes, expressions of love do not require much fanfare.
Often the simplest gesture says the most.

My husband, Chad, and I have gone through many struggles in our relationship with each other, and with our children. Yet through it all our love has grown stronger. Again and again we marvel at the gift God gave us in each other. I do not believe that our relationship could ever exist without romance – the little joys or surprises we make for each other are what confirm and renew our love time and again. I am always happily surprised when Chad, who is a writer, presents me with a poem or brings home flowers for our table. And how he loves it when I have a cup of coffee or fresh-baked cookies ready for him at the end of the day.

We have discovered that nothing is more reviving than a good laugh as we recount the day's little experiences to each other, or when he pulls my leg about something. . . . It is true that marriage is a serious commitment for life, yet I think we can also be very childlike about it and trust in God's leading, taking one step at a time. We stumble along; we make our mistakes; we have our disagreements and arguments. But afterwards we love each other all the more.

The Spirit opens up an entirely different plane of experience.

When two people seek to have a deeper, more intimate relationship, they usually do so in terms of mutual emotions, common values, shared ideas, and a feeling of goodwill toward each other. Without despising these, we must recognize that the Holy Spirit opens up an entirely different plane of experience between husband and wife.

Certainly, marital love based on the excitement of emotion can be wonderful, but it can all too quickly become desperate and unhappy. In the long run it is an unstable foundation. Love gains certainty and firmness only when it is ruled by the Spirit.

If we seek only the unity and love that is possible on a human level, we remain like clouds drifting and suspended. When we seek unity in the Spirit, God can ignite in us a faithful love that can endure to the end. The Spirit burns away everything that cannot endure. He purifies our love. True love does not originate from within ourselves, but is poured out over us.

Marriage in the Holy Spirit is a covenant of faithfulness. Where there is no loyalty, there is no true love nor real happiness. In our society, marriages are being tested as never before, but this should refine and increase our commitment to one another. Faithfulness springs from the inward certainty of our calling. It comes from a joyful submission to God's plan.

In his *Confession of Faith* (1540), the Anabaptist Peter Riedemann describes God's order for marriage as encompassing three levels. First is the marriage of God to his people, of Christ to his church, and of the Spirit to our spirit (1 Cor. 6:17). Second is the community of God's people among themselves – justice and common fellowship in spirit and soul. Third is the unity between one man and one woman (Eph. 5:31), which "is visible to and understandable by all."[14]

Unity of faith is the surest basis for marriage.

Paul the Apostle also draws a parallel between marriage and spiritual unity when he tells husbands to love their wives "just as Christ loved the church and gave himself up for her" (Eph. 5:25). For Christians, marriage is a reflection of the deepest unity: the unity of God and his church. In a Christian marriage, therefore, it is the unity of God's kingdom, in Christ and in the Holy Spirit, that matters most. Ultimately, it is the only sure foundation on which a marriage can be built. "Seek first God's kingdom and his righteousness, and all these things will be given to you as well" (Matt. 6:33).

Marriage should always lead two believing people closer to Jesus and his kingdom. It is not good enough for a couple to get married in a church or by a minister. To be drawn nearer to Christ, they must first be fully dedicated as individuals to the spirit of God's kingdom, and to the church community that serves it and stands under its direction. First there must be heartfelt unity of faith and spirit. Only then will there be true unity of soul and body as well.

This is why (at least traditionally) so many churches have been reluctant to bless the union of a member with a spouse who does not share his or her faith in Christ (2 Cor. 6:14). (In Ezra, chapters 9 and 10, we read how the prophet had to come before God and repent deeply on behalf of all the Israelites because they were marrying women from pagan nations.) On the one hand, these churches believe that anyone who is drawn by the love and justice professed by a truly Christian church will not remain an "outsider." On the other hand, they feel that a marriage between a member and a person not drawn to the church and the basic premises of its beliefs would lack the spiritual unity necessary for a secure marriage bond.

If, however, a person already married to someone of a different faith wished to join the church, I as a pastor would do my utmost to preserve the marriage, as long as the new member did not feel hindered in faith by his or her spouse.

When the love of a man and a woman who desire to be married is dedicated to the Holy Spirit and placed under his rule and direction – when it serves the unity and justice of God's kingdom – there is no reason why the two should not marry. But when a couple lacks spiritual unity, marriage in the church should be out of the question. If the church is truly the Body of Christ, the unity of its members under God must come before everything else.

Here it should be said that the demands of a godly marriage can never be met by a human system of answers or solved by means of principles, rules, and regulations. They can be grasped only in the light of God's unity, by those who have experienced his Spirit, accepted it personally, and begun to live in accordance with it.

The very essence of God's will is unity. This is why Jesus, in his last prayer, prayed that his followers would be one, just as he and the Father were one (John 17:20–23). It was God's will for unity that brought Pentecost to the world. Through the outpouring of the Spirit, people's hearts were struck, and they repented and were baptized. The fruits of their new life were not only spiritual. The material and practical aspects of their lives, too, were affected and even revolutionized. Goods were collected and sold, and the proceeds were laid at the feet of the apostles. Everyone wanted to give all they had out of love. Yet no one suffered want, and everyone received what he or she needed. Nothing was held back. There were no laws or principles to govern this revolution. Not even Jesus said exactly how it should be brought about, only,

"Sell your possessions and give to the poor" (Matt. 19:21). At Pentecost it simply happened: the Spirit descended and united the hearts and lives of those who believed (Acts 2:42–47).

*The Spirit frees us from pettiness
and brings unity of heart.*

Genuine unity, like joy or love, cannot be forced or created artificially. Only the Spirit can bring unity. Only the Spirit can free us from our pettiness and from the forces of guilt and sin that divide us from God and from each other. With our own wills we can certainly try to free ourselves from these forces, and we may be able to overcome them to a certain degree and for a certain period of time. But we should remember that ultimately only the spirit of love can overcome the flesh.

Again, we must never forget our dependence on the guidance of the Holy Spirit (Gal. 5:25). Even within a marriage, if our relationship is based only on mutual feelings or common values and not on the Spirit, it runs the risk of being swallowed up by the erotic and emotional. We ourselves are not capable of bringing about the spiritual unity in which two hearts become one. That can happen only when we allow ourselves to be gripped and transformed by something greater than ourselves.

When a marriage is anchored in the Holy Spirit, both partners will feel that their love is not a private possession but a fruit and gift of God's all-embracing love. They will still have to combat selfishness, superficiality, or other disorders, but if they keep their hearts open, the Spirit will always lift their eyes to God and his help.

The Spirit must come to each of us, whether married or unmarried, again and again. God wants to transform everything in our hearts and give us the strength to love. In his First Letter to the Corinthians, Paul says, "There is nothing love cannot face; there is no limit to its faith, its hope, and its endurance. Love will never come to an end." Love is born of the Holy Spirit, and only in the Spirit can a true marriage be conceived – and endure.

9

The Mystery of Marriage

Submit to one another out of reverence for Christ.
Wives, submit yourselves to your own husbands
as you do to the Lord. For the husband is the head
of the wife as Christ is the head of the church, his
body, of which he is the Savior. Now as the church
submits to Christ, so also wives should submit to
their husbands in everything. Husbands, love
your wives, just as Christ loved the church and
gave himself up for her to make her holy, cleansing
her by the washing with water through the word,
and to present her to himself as a radiant church,
without stain or wrinkle or any other blemish, but
holy and blameless. In this same way, husbands
ought to love their wives as their own bodies. He
who loves his wife loves himself. After all, no one
ever hated their own body, but they feed and care
for their body, just as Christ does the church – for
we are members of his body. "For this reason a man
will leave his father and mother and be united to
his wife, and the two will become one flesh." This
is a profound mystery – but I am talking about
Christ and the church.

Ephesians 5:21–32

IN GOD'S ORDER, marriage and family originate in
the church. The church is God's primary expression of

his love and justice in the world. In the church, marriage can be fulfilled and given its true value. Without the church, it is doomed to be overcome by the dominating and destructive forces of society.

Marriage is more than a bond between husband and wife.

Only very few people in our day understand that marriage contains a mystery far deeper than the bond of husband and wife – that is, the eternal unity of Christ with his people. In a true marriage, the unity of husband and wife will reflect this deeper unity. It is not only a bond between one man and one woman, because it is sealed by the greater bond of unity with God and his people. This bond must always come first. In my church, we affirm this unity at baptism and reaffirm it at every celebration of the Lord's Supper, and we remind ourselves of it at every wedding. Without it, even the happiest marriage will bear no lasting fruit.

How little the marriage covenant amounts to when it is only a promise or contract between two people! How different the state of the modern family would be if Christians everywhere were willing to place loyalty to Christ and his church above their marriages.

For those who have faith, Christ – the one who truly unites – always stands between the lover and the beloved. It is his Spirit that gives them unhindered access to one another. Therefore, when sin enters a marriage and clouds the truth of love, a faithful disciple will follow Jesus in the church, not his or her wayward spouse.

Emotional love will protest this because it is prone to disregard the truth. It may even try to hinder the clear light that comes from God. It is unable and unwilling to let go of a relationship, even when it becomes false and ungenuine. But true love never follows evil: it rejoices in the truth (1 Cor. 13:6). Both marriage partners must recognize that unity of faith is more important than the emotional bond of their marriage. Each of us who claims to be a disciple must ask ourselves: "If my first allegiance is not to Jesus and the church, who is it to?" (Luke 9:57–60)

When the smaller unity of a married couple is placed under the greater unity of the church, their marriage becomes steadfast and secure on a new, deeper level because it is placed within the unity of all believers. It is hardly surprising that this idea is foreign to most people, yet it contains a truth I have witnessed time and again. Take the story of Harry and Betty, an elderly couple I got to know well during their last years together. In Betty's words:

> Harry and I were married in June 1937, in England. Though at first we felt our marriage to be founded under God, it was not long before our struggles began. Harry, who struggled with homosexual inclinations all his life, became unfaithful to me, and then left me. Several times he tried to set things straight, but he never seemed to be able to break with the sin that bound him. During our long years of separation, close friends stood by him and me, and this was a great support.
>
> When distressing letters came from Harry, I got discouraged, and sometimes I gave up praying for him. But I always came back to it, as it was the only thing I could do to help him. I knew that with God everything is possible, and hoped that someday Harry might be restored to Christ and the church. . . .

Now I can never cease to marvel at what a miracle
it was that he returned to me in his old age. We had
not been together for over forty years. But I loved
being with him during the last years we shared; he was
so different. He was humble and straightforward and
childlike. He came to love my friends, and our neighbors, and they loved him. Harry and I read the Bible
and his favorite hymns together. He was very close to
Jesus in his final months.

I think of him every day and will always treasure
the time I had with him. I think he was closer to the
kingdom than I am. I fail in love again and again
and see too late things I could have done. But God is
faithful and keeps his promises. My faith rests in this,
and I have peace.

Betty was too modest to ever say it, but had it not been for
her constant prayer and her faithfulness to Jesus, Harry
might never have found his way back to God and to faith,
let alone back to her. Their last two years together are a
testament to faith and to the healing power of uncompromising love. What a contrast to today's culture, where
so many seem to think that the more independently a
marriage is built, the firmer it is. Some even think that
the more a couple can be relieved of the "constraints" of
obligation to each other, the happier they will be. This is
a completely false presumption. Only when a marriage is
founded in God's order and on the basis of his love can it
last. A marriage is built on sand unless it is built on the
rock of faith.

Man and woman have different tasks,
and they must complement each other.

The conviction that love to Christ and his church must take priority over all else is also important for understanding the difference between man and woman. Clearly God has given each of them different natures and tasks, and when these are rightly fulfilled in a marriage in the church, harmony and love will abound. My father, J. Heinrich Arnold, writes:

> Obviously, there are differences in the biological makeup of the male and the female. But it is completely materialistic to think that the difference between man and woman is merely biological. A woman longs to absorb her beloved one into herself. She is designed by nature to receive and to endure; to conceive, to bear, to nurse, and to protect. A man, on the other hand, desires to enter his beloved one and become one with her; he is made to initiate and penetrate rather than to receive.[15]

It has been said that the body is shaped by the soul, and this is a deep thought. The soul, the breath of God, the innermost essence of each human being, forms a different body for each. It is never a question of who is higher. Both man and woman were made in the image of God, and what can be greater than that? Yet there is a difference: Paul likens man to Christ and woman to the church (Eph. 5:22–24). Man, as head, portrays the service of Christ. Woman, as body, portrays the dedication of the church. There is a difference in calling, but there is no difference in worth.

Mary is a symbol of the church. In her we recognize the true nature of womanhood and motherhood. Woman is like the church because she receives and carries the Word within her (Luke 1:38) and brings life into the world in keeping with God's will. This is the highest thing that can be said of a human being.

A woman's love is different from a man's. It tends to be more steady, more in keeping with her loyal nature. It is dedicated to protecting and guiding all those in its care. Man's love, on the other hand, seeks others out and challenges them. It is the pioneering zeal of the apostle, of Christ's representative: Go out and gather! Teach all people. Submerge them in the atmosphere of God, in the life of God the Father, the Son, and the Holy Spirit (Matt. 28:18–20). But man's task, like woman's, is always bound together with the task of the church.

Both Paul and Peter point out that the husband is the head of his wife, not in himself but in Christ (1 Cor. 11:3). This does not mean that the man is "higher"; the fact that woman is taken from man and man is born of woman shows that they are dependent on each other in every respect (1 Cor. 11:11–12). Again, the gifts and responsibilities of one are worth no more than those of the other; they are simply different. In God's order of marriage, both husband and wife will find their rightful place, but neither will rule the other. Love and humility will rule.

It belongs to the evil of our day that both men and women avoid the responsibilities given them by God. Women rebel against the inconvenience of pregnancy and the pain of birth, and men rebel against the burden of commitment to the children they father and to the woman who bears them. Such rebellion is a curse on our time. It will lead future generations astray. Woman was designed by God to have children, and a real man will respect and love his wife all the more because of this. Peter admonishes us:

> You husbands must conduct your married life with understanding: pay honor to the woman's body, not only because it is weaker, but also because you share together in the grace of God which gives you life. Then your prayers will not be hindered (1 Pet. 3:7 NEB).

It is clear that the difference between man and woman is not absolute. In a true woman there is courageous manliness, and in a true man there is the submission and humility of Mary. Yet because the husband is the head, he will give the lead, even if he is a very weak person. This must not be taken as if man were an overlord and woman his servant. If a husband does not lead in love and humility – if he does not lead in the spirit of Jesus – his headship will become tyranny. The head has its place in the body, but it does not dominate.

When I marry a couple, I always ask the bridegroom if he is willing to lead his wife "in everything that is good," which simply means to lead her more deeply to Jesus. In the same way, I ask the bride if she is willing to follow her husband. It is simply a matter of both of them following Jesus together.

True leadership means loving service.

In his letter to the Ephesians, Paul points to the self-sacrificing love that lies in true leadership: "Husbands, love your wives, just as Christ loved the church and gave himself up for her" (Eph. 5:25). This task, the task of loving, is actually the task of every man and woman, whether married or not.

When we take Paul's words to heart, we will experience the true inner unity of a relationship ruled by love – an inner speaking of the heart to God from both spouses together. Only then will God's blessing rest on our marriages. We will constantly seek our beloved one anew and continually look for ways to serve each other in love. Most wonderful of all, we will find everlasting joy. As the church father Tertullian writes:

Who can describe the happiness of a marriage contracted in the presence of the church and sealed with its blessing? What a sweet yoke it is which here joins two believing people in one hope, one way of life, one vow of loyalty, and one service to God! They are brother and sister, both busy in the same service, with no separation of soul and body, but as two in one flesh. And where there is one flesh, there is one spirit also. Together they pray, together they kneel down: the one teaches the other, and bears with the other. They are joined together in the church of God, joined at the Lord's table, joined in anxiety, persecution, and recovery. They vie with each other in the service of their Lord. Christ sees and hears, and joyfully does he send them his peace, for where two are gathered together in his name, there is he in the midst of them.[16]

10

The Sacredness of Sex

Marriage should be honored by all, and the marriage bed kept pure, for God will judge the adulterer and all the sexually immoral.

Hebrews 13:4

THERE ARE TWO DANGERS in sex: on the one hand, fear of the self-surrender or closeness that a physical relationship requires, and fear that sex is dirty and shameful; on the other, unbridled lust and sin. Clearly, the sexual sphere is not incorruptible. Even in marriage its potential blessings become dangers if it is entered in isolation from God, who created it. Instead of passion there is naked lust, instead of tenderness there is aggression and even brutality, and instead of mutual self-giving there is uncontrollable desire.

The church should never be silent about this (1 Cor. 5:1–5). The spirit of impurity is always waiting to tempt us, and it will slip into the sanctuary of marriage whenever we open the door to it. Once impurity has entered a marriage, it becomes more and more difficult to keep focused on God's love, and easier and easier to bypass one another and succumb to evil temptations.

We must never underestimate the power of the impure spirits that drive people to do evil, even within marriage. Once under their control, sex quickly loses its nobler qualities and deteriorates into something cheap. What was created as a wonderful gift from God becomes a sinister, life-destroying experience. Only repentance can bring about healing and restoration.

Through sexual union,
an unparalleled uniting can take place.

We can recognize the true nature of the sexual sphere most clearly when we can see its sacredness as the fulfillment of wedded love sanctioned by God. It is the same with the act of sexual intercourse itself, the moment in which marital love comes to its fullest physical expression. Because intercourse is such a powerfully dramatic experience, it is vital that it be anchored in God. If sex is not recognized as a gift from God and subordinated to him, it can become an idol. Entered with reverence, however, it "awakens that which is most intimate, most sacred, most vulnerable in the human heart."[17]

In a true marriage, sex is guided by more than the desires of each partner: it is guided by the love that binds both of them together. When both partners give themselves in complete surrender to the other, a uniting of unparalleled depth takes place. It will not be just "physical love"; it will be the expression and fulfillment of total love, an act of unconditional giving and deep fulfillment.

It is a remarkable and wonderful experience to give oneself physically to another person. Orgasm, the climax or peak of physical uniting, is a powerful and shaking experience and has a forceful effect on the spirit. Here, the experience of the body is so forceful that it is difficult to distinguish it from the experience of the spirit. In rhythmic harmony of heart and body, two human beings reach the highest peak of the joy of love. In total union, both are lifted out of their own personalities and joined in the closest community possible. At the moment of climax a person is, so to speak, swept away – engulfed so completely that the sense of being an independent person is momentarily submerged.

Physical union should always express
unity of heart and soul.

We can never have too much reverence for the act of sexual intercourse. Even if we reject prudishness, a feeling of reticence will make us wary of speaking about it to others. Of course, a man and woman united in marriage must be able to talk openly with each other, even about the most intimate things. But they will never do this without the reverence that springs from their love for each other.

It is of prime importance that a couple does not go to bed at night without having turned first to Jesus. It is not necessary to use many words; Jesus always knows what we mean and what we need. We must not only thank him but also seek his guidance – if we do not knock at his door, he cannot guide us. The same, of course, is true at the beginning of the day.

If our marriage is grounded in Jesus and his love and purity, we will find the right relationship to each other on every level. Here we must heed Paul's warning, "In your anger do not sin: Do not let the sun go down while you are still angry, and do not give the devil a foot-hold" (Eph. 4:26–27). Prayer is crucial in reconciling the differences that arise in the marriage relationship. To unite physically when there is no unity of heart is hypocrisy. It is a desecration of the bond of love.

Physical uniting should always express the full uniting of spirit and soul; it should never be a means of bodily satisfaction alone. In Jesus, every physical act of love is a mutual giving of self, a sign of resolve to live for one another. It has nothing to do with power or the idea of sex as conquest.

Anyone who uses his spouse merely to satisfy himself insults his own dignity and the dignity of his partner. He is using sex for a selfish purpose. This is why the Bible regards it as sin when a man withdraws from his wife before climax and allows his semen to "fall on the ground" (Gen. 38:9–10). Of course, if this happens against his will, prematurely, or in a dream, then it is not a sin. For the same reason, oral and anal intercourse are also sinful. Because they are driven only by the selfish desire for sexual excitement, these forms of sex are in reality forms of mutual masturbation.

True sexual fulfillment is found in mutual submission.

Sexual desire may be relatively dormant in a newly married couple, especially when neither spouse has engaged in premarital sex or been addicted to masturbation. In fact, a husband may even need to awaken the urge for intercourse in his bride. Because this may take time, he should be very patient and initiate sexual union only when his wife is ready. For a virgin, the first intercourse can be painful and may cause minor bleeding. This is no cause for alarm, yet a husband should be aware of his wife's discomfort.

A loving husband will have enough care for his wife to consider her state of readiness and not hurry intercourse because of his own impatience. Because he is concerned not merely with his own satisfaction, he will be sensitive to the fact that often more time is needed for a woman to reach climax than for a man, and after intercourse, he will not go happily to sleep while his wife lies awake with feelings of deep disappointment or frustration.

The sexual happiness of a woman is often more dependent than a man's on the accompanying circumstances of their union; on the closeness she feels between herself and her husband, and in little acts of kindness or affectionate words. It does not consist only in the climax. Simply being together with her beloved may give her the deepest sense of fulfillment.

A couple should learn how to prepare one another for physical union. Loving stimulation is a strong affirmation of mutual unity, and in addition to increasing readiness, it nurtures confidence and envelops a couple in a feeling of security. Both husband and wife must learn what pleases and arouses their partner. Writing about women, for instance, von Gagern says, "There are areas of the body that are especially responsive to fondling – the mouth, the breasts, under the arms, the spine – but a couple's own unique love for each other will continually guide them anew."[18]

As self-discipline, abstinence can deepen a couple's love.

Physically, intercourse is always possible, but a husband should be ready to abstain for the sake of his wife's health, especially before and after she gives birth. As a marriage counselor I have always recommended abstinence during menstruation and for at least six weeks before the birth of a child. I also recommend that couples abstain as long as they are able after a birth, so that the mother can recover both physically and emotionally. Because every couple is different, it is hard to suggest a time frame; the important thing is consideration. If a husband is truly considerate of his wife, he will be willing to discipline himself by abstaining as long as possible (1 Thess. 4:3–5). In such times of abstinence, out of love for her husband, the woman must be careful not to arouse him sexually.

Naturally, the love between husband and wife – between two who live together, sleep together, and belong together – will make it much harder for them to abstain than for a single person. All the more, they must be on guard against coming close to one another in a sexual way and then avoiding intercourse.

One unfounded but prevalent idea is that abstinence must be fundamentally negative or frustrating. If born out of love, it can actually create a deeper, more enriching relationship. It can even have a healing affect. John Kippley, the founder of a national ministry to couples, tells how a woman he knows who was abused by her father experienced healing through her husband's consideration of her needs. "Because of his restraint," she told John, "I was able to discover for the first time that I was more than my body. I could be loved without having to perform sexually. I had true value as a person, not just as an object of satisfaction."

As a woman approaches middle-age, it is not unusual for her joy or interest in sexual intercourse to diminish.

This can be difficult for her husband, yet he must see that his love for his wife does not decrease. The wife, for her part, should give herself in love to her husband as she is able, even if her joy in doing so is not the same as it was in earlier years (1 Cor. 7:3–4). Otherwise a husband may be tempted to seek other outlets for his sexual impulses. The main thing is that there is always unity of spirit and soul before physical uniting and that, when abstinence is necessary, it does not become an occasion for love to grow cold. Paul writes:

> Do not deprive each other except by mutual consent and for a time, so that you may devote yourselves to prayer. Then come together again so that Satan will not tempt you because of your lack of self-control (1 Cor. 7:5).

Abstinence, then, may be best approached with fasting and prayer – as a self-discipline. When willingly accepted in this way, it can unite a couple more deeply than ever.

In the end, everything in a marriage depends on the commitment of both partners to Jesus and on their willingness to follow his leading. Couples should remember that it was God who joined them together, and only he can keep them together, especially in difficult times. Jesus says, "Whoever loses his life will gain it" (Luke 9:24). The same is true in Christian marriage: insofar as both partners are willing to give themselves again and again to each other and to Christ, they will find the true fulfillment of unity and freedom.

II

Parenthood
and the Gift of Children

*Children, obey your parents in the Lord, for this is
right. "Honor your father and mother" – which is
the first commandment with a promise – "so that it
may go well with you and that you may enjoy long
life on the earth." Fathers, do not exasperate your
children; instead, bring them up in the training
and instruction of the Lord.*

Ephesians 6:1–4

WE LIVE IN A WORLD where the structure of family
life is undergoing profound changes, in rich and poor
countries alike. The concept of family as a stable, cohesive
unit is fast becoming lost. We are even afraid to define
what a family is because we do not want to offend anyone.

For years, psychologists have warned of the effects of
broken marriages, teen pregnancies, violent homes, and
other social ills, but their warnings have been given in
vain. Now we are reaping a bitter harvest. All this makes
it more urgent than ever for us to rediscover God's original intent in creating man and woman, and in blessing
them with children.[19]

Having children today requires courage.

Modern society despises the family. It is difficult for a family with several children to find a house, and in many places it is impossible to rent an apartment, even if there is only one child. Children are simply not wanted. Many people think it regrettable to leave jobs or other pursuits to have children, and they often look down on women who choose to stay at home to raise children instead of pursuing a more "acceptable" career.

Having children in these times certainly takes great courage, but that is what faith means: not knowing what lies ahead, and yet still trusting that God has his hand over all things and will have the final say. More than ever, parents need to trust God. The health of a society (and the health of any church or movement within society) depends on the strength of its marriages. Where there is reverence for God, there are strong and stable families, but as soon as this is lost, there is rapid disintegration and decline.

Those who know what it means to see a child smile for the first time, to love him or her, and to feel love in return know something of the greatness of God and the nearness of eternity in each child. They know that their child is like no other, and that no child could replace this one in their hearts. They will also realize what an awe-inspiring responsibility it is to bring a child into the world – a responsibility that only grows with the child – and will sense that they are too weak and sinful to bring up even one child in their own strength.

But our recognition of inadequacy should not lead us to despair. It should make us realize how dependent we are on grace. Only the adult who stands like a child before the grace of God is fit to raise a child.

On what basis should a family be built?

If we think of starting a family, our first question should be: on what foundation? Complete dedication to Christ and his church is the only dependable foundation. On him alone can we build a rich and fulfilled family life that will withstand the forces that attack it.

It is the task of every couple to bring up their children in God's stead, to represent the creator. For the small child especially, father and mother stand for God. That is why the commandment to honor father and mother is so vital to the upbringing of every child from the start. Without it, the commandment to honor God has no real meaning for the child. Actually, every child has an instinctive longing for the security of father, mother, and God. It is terrible, then, when parents do not fulfill this longing, when they see parenting merely as a role and are not truly fathers or mothers. Children will sense such hypocrisy wherever it occurs, and they will become resentful, bitter, and rebellious as they grow older.

The same is true if a couple lives in dissension – if a wife does not support her husband's task as head of the family, for example, or if a husband does not love and honor his wife. When children cannot see a picture of God in their parents, they have trouble finding a secure and healthy foundation for their later lives. They may even experience emotional difficulties.

I once counseled a family I had known since their four children were very young. The parents had all the right intentions, yet they were divided over whose role it was to lead the family. While friends and neighbors were presented with a peaceful enough picture, within the family tensions and rivalry developed. As their children grew up, the parents were too disunited to lead them properly, and thereby set a poor example for them to follow.

Now their children are adults. They are all lovable, bright, and talented, yet they are floundering. Because their parents never dealt with the elements of mistrust and disunity in their marriage, these young adults now find it very hard to trust anyone. Like their parents, it is difficult for them to be sincere and honest with themselves, and they always need to feel in control. Sadly, they don't realize how this cuts them off from other people, and they have become lonely and disillusioned. Worst of all, they are wholly unrealistic in their expectations and seem to think the world owes them success.

It is of greatest importance that from the first day of a child's life he or she is surrounded by love and by reverence for God. To the same degree that children experience the love their parents have for each other, they will find the inner security they need in order to develop and grow.

In questions of discipline, a husband and wife should do their utmost to be fully agreed as to what they expect in terms of behavior. Children should not have to decide which parent is right. Their position should be one of trust, not judgment. They look for consistent boundaries and for the security that comes from unity, love, and mutual respect. These things are the basis of true love for children.

Children need living examples, not religious words.

The first five years of a child's life are the most formative, and therefore the best time for parents to bring Jesus and the gospel alive to their children. This can be done quite simply by telling them about Jesus' birth, death, and resurrection. All these things can move the hearts of children at a surprisingly young age and awaken in them a love for God and for Jesus.

We cannot bring our children to Jesus, however, if he is only a figure in our Bibles. Children will always want to come to Jesus, but they will instinctively rebel against false piety. As Blumhardt once put it, "If we try to drag children into the kingdom by means of our religiosity, they will flee from our pious homes as fast as they are able."[20] Therefore we should be careful not to put our children under any religious pressure or plague them with talk about sins they can neither understand nor commit. We want them to have a childlike attitude toward God, toward Jesus, and toward the Bible. It is of no use, for instance, to make children learn even the shortest passages of Scripture if God does not speak directly into their little hearts. Rather than try to "teach" children faith, it is much better for their parents to live their faith by example in a spontaneous, genuine way. When our children see that we, their parents, rely on God for everything – when they see us thank him and obey his commands – they will feel an inner urge to pray and to follow him of their own accord.

Our task is to guide our children, not control them.

Raising children requires daily discipline, but we should never forget that caring for them in God's stead means guiding, not controlling, them. Children must be encouraged to overcome themselves and look beyond their little worlds from a very early age, and they must learn to love and respect others. They cannot be left to swing with every mood and follow every selfish whim without restraint. Clear directions and consistent boundaries are always necessary. In fact, discipline is the greatest love we can show them (Heb. 12:10–11). But it is not love to coerce them or crush their spirit.

We must remember that every child is a thought of God (Ps. 139:13–17) and try to understand why it is said that "a little child will lead them" (Isa. 11:6). In guiding our children, we cannot and should not try to shape them according to our own intentions or plans. We should not force on them anything that has not been born into them, awakened from within, or given them by God. God has a specific intent for each child; he has a plan for every one, and he will hold to it. Our task is to help each child find God's purpose for him and fulfill it.

Carrying out this task means continually exercising self-denial in our own human efforts to lead a child. Sometimes, it may mean refraining from tearing children away from their own thoughts. Blumhardt notes how quickly we hurt our relationship with children when we interrupt their thoughts and happy disposition and attempt to influence them with our ideas or advice: "When left undisturbed, children learn obedience and respect best of all."[21]

Naturally, we must be on guard against permissiveness. Flabbiness is often a fruit of an unhealthy emotionalism between parent and child. It inhibits the childlike spirit because it subjects the child to the spinelessness of an adult who has lost the clarity of Christ. We must always watch that our children are free from such false ties.

True authority strengthens and stimulates a child.

Children must never feel ill-used if spoken to or admonished sharply. They need to learn to take themselves in hand and face up to what has happened when they are shown to be in the wrong. They should not give half-answers that could mean this or that. Yet even if a certain sharpness toward children is healthy, impatience is not, especially when it results in corporal punishment. That, Eberhard Arnold writes, is a "declaration of bankruptcy."

Parents must reject both the harshness of physical punishment and the power of manipulation: both are forms of authoritarianism that fail to take the child seriously as a bearer of God's image. The one fails in mercy, and the other in honesty. Both fail in love. True authority stimulates and strengthens what is good in each child by leading him to make his own decisions between right and wrong. Only when we lead children with trust and love will they feel the desire to struggle against the evil that tries to work in them and in each of us.

I thank God that I had a father who could be very firm with us children when necessary. Like any child, I rebelled at times against his strictness, but I always knew it was a sign of his love for me. From early childhood on, our parents instilled in us children the value of the fifth commandment, to honor father and mother. We knew that if we did not love and honor them, we were actually dishonoring God.

As for my mother, my father insisted that we children show her respect. He would not tolerate disobedience to her. Only in later years did I realize his wisdom. It is the father's task to uphold respect toward the mother, since she carries the weightier burden in raising their children, especially when they are small, or sick.

Though my father could be stern, I never once felt threatened by him. Whenever he reprimanded me for doing something wrong, I could count on his complete forgiveness and love once I had accepted my responsibility and wanted to make amends. I knew that the wrong I had done would be forgotten, and that I would be able to make a fresh start.

My father showed me the significance of loving authority, an authority that only God can give. In each child's heart is a longing to hear a "no" when a "no" is needed, and a desire to set things right when he knows he has done something wrong. True parental authority gives inner security to a child, because it provides the child with the stability of set boundaries.

Most fathers and mothers do not intentionally mislead their children, and if they do misguide them without meaning to, they are likely to suffer the consequences along with their children. Some parents are confident about their child-rearing abilities, and others are not, but there are times when both will throw up their hands. When this is the case, it is vital that they find the humility to ask someone for help – whether a close friend,

a relative, a teacher, or a trusted pastor or family counselor. Of course, help must be enlisted in such a way that it
reassures the child in question – and not at the expense of
a relationship with him or her. Even the best expert assis-
tance may, at the end of the day, be a hindrance – not a
help. I say this because ultimately, "successful" parenting
is not a matter of capability or wisdom, but of grace. My
father writes in this regard:

> Christ calls us to become like children, and this means
> we must drop everything and become completely depen-
> dent on God and on one another. If we as parents love
> God with all our heart and soul, our children will have
> the right reverence for us, and we will also have rever-
> ence for our children and for the wonderful mystery of
> becoming and being a child. Reverence for the spirit that
> moves between parent and child is the basic element of a
> happy family life.[22]

12

The Purity of Childhood

Therefore, whoever takes the lowly position of this child is the greatest in the kingdom of heaven. And whoever welcomes one such child in my name welcomes me. "If anyone causes one of these little ones – those who believe in me – to stumble, it would be better for them to have a large millstone hung around their neck and to be drowned in the depths of the sea.

Matthew 18:4–6

JESUS' WORDS TELL US what great value the soul of a little child has in the eyes of God. Spiritually, every child is close to the throne of God, to the heart of God, and every child has a guardian angel who always sees the face of the Father in heaven (Matt. 18:10).

When a baby comes into the world it is as though he or she brings the pure air of heaven along. At every birth we feel that something of God is born, that something of eternity has come down to us. The innocence of a child is an enormous blessing.

The childlike spirit must be protected – but also nurtured.

In spite of the innocence of every child, however, there is also an inclination to sin in each one (Ps. 51:5). That is why it is such a terrible thing to lead a child astray. Children are corrupted not only by intentionally misleading them to sin, but by exposing them to anything that violates the atmosphere of innocence around them and deprives them of their childlikeness. So many of the images to which children are exposed today – on television and the internet, at shopping malls, and at school – are created by adults obsessed with sex, violence, power, and money. Is it any wonder that children lose their childlike spirit and childhood itself?

The best thing we can do for our children is to ensure that the whole atmosphere in which they live is filled with the spirit of purity and ruled by love. The inner education of children – the task of leading them to respect and to love God, their parents, their teachers, and everyone around them – is a holy privilege. Here it is of utmost importance that we pray for God's spirit to arouse our children's wills for what is pure, genuine, and good. Guiding children to do what is good is far more important than teaching them to recite verses or to say prayers which may not come from the heart. That is why my church avoids formal religious instruction as such. We feel that children can learn to love God best through simple songs, stories from the Bible, and the daily example of adults around them who love each other.

In leading children to Jesus it is important that we ourselves have a childlike attitude toward his command-ments and sayings, toward the angel-world, and toward the Bible as a whole. How very quickly and simply chil-dren take these things into their hearts!

We can also bring our children to God through the world around them, by helping them to sense him in all they see – in sun, moon, and stars; birds and animals; trees and flowers; mountains and thunderstorms. Children instinctively want to live in nature and with nature, and in every child there is a love for the earth, a joy in the starry sky, and a warm fondness for everything living. To a child, the world of God and his angels is often much closer and more real than we suspect.

Through nature and through the Bible, children will encounter suffering and death at an early age. While it is important for us to teach them to have a heart for those who suffer, it is equally important not to burden or frighten them. In general, too many facts about the cycle of life – of reproduction, birth, and death – can harm a child's inner experience of God's world. Birth and death are mysteries that can only be understood in relationship to God, and there is danger of irreverence in saying too much.

In this respect, we need to have a greater awe and reverence for pregnancy and childbirth. It is not without reason that Jesus compares the end times and the coming of a new world with a mother in labor, and the tremendous joy of the new life after all the pain and agony. Whenever a couple is expecting a child, a deep mystery is present. We can do great inward harm whenever we talk lightly or joke about pregnancy or draw too much attention to it. A quiet, humble anticipation will instill a natural reverence in children for God's gift of new life.

Concerning sex, especially, it is not necessary for a child or even an adolescent to know everything. It is all too easy to destroy our children's sense of the sacredness and mystery of life with too much discussion and exposure. Today as never before, parents must be alert to the insidious dangers of our sex-crazed culture, which can all too easily infiltrate our homes through what we and our children see, hear, and read.

I am not in any way suggesting that children be brought up ignorant of the basic facts of life. I only mean that these things should never be separated from the world of God. The main thing is that we do not disturb the purity of childhood – the natural relationship of every child to his or her creator.

Education means rousing a child
to choose right over wrong.

To protect the purity of children means to win them for the good. It is wrong to suppose that a child is not tempted to sin. As parents we must always be ready to fight evil in our children, whether it takes the form of lying, stealing, disrespect, or sexual impurity. But we must do this without too many rules (Col. 2:20–22). Moralism, which always involves suspicion and mistrust, ruins the childlike spirit. Obedience is never enough. Compliance alone does not build a child's character. On the one hand, children cannot be left unprotected to fall prey to whatever evil comes their way. On the other hand, we should not discourage them by constantly haranguing them about their faults. True education does not mean molding or squelching a child with constant criticism. It means rousing him or her to choose right over wrong.

We must be careful not to spoil our children even from an early age. Spoiling leads to selfishness, lack of self-control, and deep discontent; in other words, it leads to sin. Parents who spoil their children often confuse love with emotionalism. They think they will win their children by clinging to them, but in actual fact they only hinder them from developing into healthy, independent beings. To treat one's children as one's emotional property is to lack reverence for them as images of God in their own right.

Among older children, disrespect toward peers, educators, and parents is not uncommon. Disrespect shows itself in many ways. Among boys it may take the form of machismo (which is mostly a cover-up for cowardice, and is only displayed when others are present) or a lack of consideration for others, or irreverent or destructive behavior. Singing may be despised as effeminate, signs of affection to babies may be scoffed at, and everything religious or moral is apt to be mocked. Among girls disrespect often shows itself in cruel gossip or backbiting, secrecy, and over-sensitivity to criticism.

Because children who demonstrate such tendencies are insecure, they are susceptible to peer pressure and will often turn to the support of a clique. Parents and teachers need to be alert to this, because the exclusive nature of even the friendliest clique is never healthy. The best antidote to cliquishness is positive guidance, care, and genuine interest in each child.

Every child instinctively longs for a good conscience.

The question of sexual impurity in children needs special sensitivity and discernment. My father writes:

How to fight against sin in children is a very difficult question. If there are indecencies, for example, which mostly begin with children exposing themselves to each other and sometimes touching each other, the child will feel instinctively that this is not right. These indecencies almost always involve lying. We must be careful not to make too much of such things among children. It may only draw their attention to the sexual area all the more. The best thing, perhaps, is to admonish them and so close the matter, and then help them to think of other things.

We grown-ups too easily forget that many things do not mean the same to a child as they do to us, and we must never project our ideas and feelings and experiences onto a child's mind (Titus 1:15). We must also never forget that it is in a certain way natural for children to go through periods of sexual curiosity. This cannot be mistaken for sin. But we should lead our children in such a way that their souls remain pure and innocent. Too much questioning can harm a child, because through fear he or she may become more and more entangled in lies.

It is a great injustice to label children or adolescents, especially those who have offended in the sexual area. In our assessment of childish offenses, we should beware of coming too quickly to harsh conclusions about a child's character or future development. Rather, we should help him or her to find new interests and to make a joyful new beginning.

We know that we can find the way to the heart of any child by appealing to the conscience. Every child has an instinctive, heartfelt longing for a pure conscience, and we should support this longing so that he or she does not suffer from a burdened conscience.

There is a certain point at which children are no longer children in the true sense of the word. The moment they sin consciously, they cease to be children.

It is then the task of parents and teachers to help them find repentance, the experience of Jesus on the cross, and a conversion that leads to the forgiveness of sins. Through the cross a lost childhood can be restored.[23]

Purity, like impurity, is learned by example.

For parents, the importance of seeking a relationship of trust with their children from earliest childhood cannot be emphasized enough. We cannot wait for problems that may only arise around the age of five or six. If we do not build relationships with our children while they are still young, we may never gain the trust and respect necessary to solve the more serious problems that will come with adolescence.

The years between thirteen and twenty-one are especially crucial, of course, since it is during these years that children become increasingly aware of their sexuality. How easy it is for parents – and whole churches – to turn a blind eye to the teenagers right in front of them and to fail them miserably simply by ignoring them. How different our high schools and youth centers would be if parents took time for their teenagers! Plenty of parents warn them about alcohol, drugs, and the dangers of sexual experimentation, but how many take time on a regular basis to guide their children's interests and encourage them to use their time creatively? Committed parents will remain in close touch with their children throughout the ups and downs of adolescence. Fathers will be not only fathers to their children – they will be comrades and friends as well; mothers will be the same.

Young people always need someone to confide in. Whether it is a parent, pastor, counselor, or friend, there must be someone they trust with whom they can freely share their joys or struggles, and with whom they can talk openly about sex without shame or embarrassment.

Today's teenagers are simply presented with too many options. Our culture believes variety is the key to freedom and fulfillment; but in actual fact, it may be the key to confusion. Too few people are willing to warn teenagers of the painful emotional scars that follow on the heels of uncommitted sexual activity. There are even fewer who are able to point them to the hope of forgiveness after they have failed.

For this reason, trusted role models are especially needed. Children spend more time than ever on their own; across the social spectrum, latchkey kids are increasingly common. It is no accident that today's children have been dubbed by some experts as "Generation Alone," or that studies assign words like "abandoned," or "alienated" to describe them.

Lest we forget, purity, like impurity, is learned first and foremost by example (Titus 2:6–8). Children need to see that the love between their parents is indissoluble, and to know that certain looks, touches, and words of affection are appropriate only between a married man and woman. They need to see that physical intimacy belongs to marriage alone and that experimentation of any sort beforehand will only stain a later marriage. They certainly need to be spared the confusion and pain of broken relationships and sexual sin in or among adults around them.

That is why it is so important that the church has a central place in family life. Children must be able to see living examples of purity not only in their parents, but in everyone around them, whether married or single.

The best safeguard against sin is love.

Purity cannot be fostered in a vacuum. Children and youth need to gain a heart for Jesus and his cause of peace and social justice. When their hearts are filled with God and inspired for his cause, they will instinctively react against evil. When we lead them to recognize the needs of others, they will long to reach out in love. The idea that children have no social conscience, no feeling for the suffering, injustice, and guilt of our world, is simply not true – this can only happen if they are brought up in an artificial environment that revolves around their own comfort and pleasure. When genuine children come face to face with the need of others, or when they see others reaching out to the needy, they will have an inner urge to extend their own love in practical ways.

The best safeguard against sin is always love. Love binds together all the virtues in perfect unity (Col. 3:14). Love is the message we need to bring to our children and youth, most importantly by demonstrating love in everything we ourselves say and do. So many young people today live for themselves and for their own interests. They work hard to get good grades, to excel in sports, to win the recognition earned by a scholarship – all of which is commendable. But how many of them care about their neighbors or the misery of the world around them? We need to challenge and stretch our youth to interact with others less fortunate than themselves.

Often parents try to protect their teenagers by anxiously shielding them from situations of impurity or violence. Yet perhaps what they really need is the opposite: the opportunity to stand on their own feet and witness to what they themselves – not just their parents – believe.

Children need to reach out and learn what others of their time are thinking and feeling, including those from different religious backgrounds. They need to relate to their peers and to the burning social, political, and economic issues of their day. They need to have a heart for the despair of those who have turned to drugs and alcohol, and for those who suffer from abusive relationships in the home. Without the ability to understand and relate to others outside their sphere, they will have no real connection to the world around them and may never be given the opportunity to test their own convictions.

We will not raise perfect children, but I firmly believe that it is possible to raise children who will respond to our guidance and discipline, in spite of the terrible corruption and darkness of our age (Prov. 22:6). As long as we are able to maintain a relationship of mutual respect and reverence, we will find the way forward with our children. It will cost a fight, sometimes a serious one, yet for the sake of a child's soul a battle is always worthwhile. Naturally, our children may grow up to choose a path of life different from that which we would have chosen for them. But if we pray to Jesus for his guidance every day, we can be confident that he will lead us and them.

13

For Those Considering Marriage

Train yourself to be godly. For physical training is
of some value, but godliness has value for all things,
holding promise for both the present life and the
life to come. . . . Don't let anyone look down on you
because you are young, but set an example for the
believers in speech, in conduct, in love, in faith, and
in purity.

1 Timothy 4:7–8, 12

IT IS TRAGIC how casually, and with what selfishness and naiveté, young men and women today plunge into relationships and even into marriage. Yet how should young people handle the natural attractions and friendships that develop between them? What is the godly approach? How can young men and women stay clear of the superficial eroticism of our time and find truly free and natural relationships? And how can they best prepare themselves for the responsibilities and demands of marriage?

Conventional dating cheapens the meaning
of commitment.

We should rejoice when there are friendships between young men and women, and when there are opportunities for positive mutual exchanges in their daily lives. To have fear of what might go wrong among them is often unwarranted, and a sign of mistrust. Young people need opportunities to relate to each other in group settings where they can work, share, sing, or relax together. To pair off or form exclusive relationships is unhealthy and out of place: in the church, young men and women should get to know each other first as brothers and sisters in Christ. They must have the freedom to be seen together without being subjected to all sorts of gossip or speculation about their friendship. The pressure caused by such talk inhibits freedom. It skews and undermines everything that is good in a relationship.

It is typical of the immaturity of a young person to "fall in love" first with one and then with another, like a bee going from flower to flower. It is only natural to want to search for "the right one"; but the church cannot tolerate the continual forming and then dissolving of new relationships. The casual attitude of a young man or woman who flits from one partner to the next is never right. It dulls the conscience and cheapens the meaning of commitment. The waves of emotional attraction that accompany every friendship between a boy and a girl are perfectly normal, but if they are not placed under Christ, they can leave wounds that may last a lifetime.

Because of this, my church rejects conventional dating. For the most part, dating in our society has become a game – a ritual of pairing off with a boyfriend or a girl-friend on the basis of physical and emotional attraction. It is built on a false understanding of friendship and often has little to do with genuine love or faithfulness. In many instances, dating is centered on an unhealthy preoccupation with personal "image." And when it involves physical or sexual intimacy, it can leave a conscience so heavily burdened that it takes years to heal.

Vanity and superficiality go hand in hand with conventional dating. So does flirting – drawing attention to oneself so as to sexually attract another person. Flirting demonstrates inner insecurity and unhappiness, and it is an insult to God.

In recent years more and more parents and churches are seeking alternatives to conventional dating. Some, for instance, are reviving the "old-fashioned" practice of courtship, which emphasizes mentoring, familial involvement, and character-enriching activities.

Unfortunately, while statistics show that dating on college campuses is on the decline, an alarming number of students are simply "hooking up," engaging in casual sex for instant gratification with no strings attached. This should spur parents, pastors, and church leaders to become even more active and involved.

*Mutual feelings are not sufficient for
building a lasting relationship.*

How should a young man or woman find the right person to marry? For a Christian the decisive factor should always be unity of heart and soul in the Spirit. Both individuals must feel that their relationship leads them closer to Jesus, for his will alone can bring together two people who are meant for each other. Without Jesus and the special unity he gives between two people, a couple will very likely not survive the storms and struggles that are a part of every marriage, especially once they have children.

Even when a couple is sure that they want to enter a more committed relationship, through engagement, for instance, they should test their love for a time to see whether it is merely the straw fire of romantic attraction, or whether there is something deeper. Again, physical and emotional attractions are natural, but they do not provide sufficient ground on which to marry or found a family, and can never be the deciding factors in making a commitment. A relationship based only on these is a shallow one, and eventually it will go to pieces. The real question should always be, "What does God want for our life and future together?" His will is the surest basis.

All of us have heard the saying, "It's what's on the inside that counts," but whether we truly believe it is another matter. Consciously or subconsciously, we have all judged other people on the basis of their physical appearance. In a culture where it is normal to hear someone say, "She's a very attractive young lady," or, "He's the good-looking one," and so on, it never hurts to think about the subtle message we are sending to those who are not described in this way.

The issue of judging people by their looks is especially important for young people considering marriage. A young woman may single out the most handsome guy around; or a young man, the prettiest girl in the bunch. But what about their relationship ten or twenty years down the road? Will they still love each other when he goes bald, when she gets wrinkles or gains weight? Certainly physical attraction is a part of every relationship, but it can never be the basis for a life-long commitment of loyalty and love. As Isaiah put it, "All flesh is grass, and all its beauty is like the flower of the field. The grass withers, the flower fades. . . ." (Isa. 40:6–7 RSV).

It is not easy to see with the eyes of the heart, particularly when we are young. Yet we must ask God to give us this special sight. If we open our hearts to his wisdom, we will see beauty in every person we meet, and love each one as a fellow being created in the image of God.

I have known Rose ever since she was a young girl. As an adult, she met and fell in love with Tom. Tom is severely crippled by cerebral palsy and has spent his entire life in a wheelchair; all the same they married and now have two lovely children. To Rose, Tom is the most wonderful man in the world. Others may see only his disabilities, but Rose sees the beauty of his soul.

Victor and Hilda, a British-born couple from my community, lived into their nineties. Married in their twenties, they remained deeply in love to the end. Hilda was not beautiful in the worldly sense: by her seventies she was severely stooped, and a nervous twitch disfigured the right side of her face. Yet to Victor, she was always "my princess." Their love was grounded in something far deeper than appearance.

During the forty years I have spent counseling young couples, many have shared their joys and struggles with me, but I am still touched every time a young person turns to me in trust. Not long ago a young woman wrote to my wife to tell her about her deepening friendship with a certain man. Kate and Andy are both members of our church and participate in our young-adult group. They are not special people, but as their relationship continues to develop, a special gift is being given to them – a firm footing for their shared seeking. Kate writes:

> From the start this has been an intensely inner experience, and we have grown very close, especially through reading the Bible and praying together. I would say, though, that the biggest struggle has been to give up our romantic, emotional idea of love, because it really has so little place. Occasionally our conversation has gotten on the level of human attractions, and the effect of that is devastating because it undermines what we have experienced together on an inner, spiritual level.... But when we keep God in the center, we find each other's hearts much more deeply.
>
> As we learn to know each other better, and know each other's day-to-day struggles and failings, we are also able to admonish and encourage each other. As a result, we both feel closer to God. More and more clearly I see how a relationship is not established once and for all, but that it must be built on a daily basis – brick by brick – and with a faith that is constant. I am so thankful for the time Andy and I are sharing together, so that we can really establish a firm foundation. And I am also grateful that it has not all been smooth sailing, because nothing worthwhile comes without a struggle.

Andy and Kate's story is heartening: even in our time it is still possible for young people to take their relationship to each other so seriously that they seek to find God above all else.

If faith is the only firm foundation for Christian marriage, it follows that each partner must make a commitment to Christ and the church before making a commitment to each other. Here the importance of baptism cannot be emphasized enough. As a confession of repentance for sin and as the covenant of a clear conscience with God, baptism is one of the greatest gifts a person can experience. I would even say that without it, there is no secure foundation for a Christian marriage.

Of course, no one should be baptized for the sake of husband, wife, or children (Luke 14:26). Nor should the desire for baptism be mixed with feelings of desire for a potential marriage partner. If baptism is to have real meaning, it must be the seal of deep repentance, conversion, and faith.

A healthy relationship needs time and care.

Jesus says that we cannot serve two masters (Matt. 6:24). He teaches us that when we trust God alone, and trust him completely, he will provide for all our needs, including the need for a partner. "Seek first his kingdom and his righteousness, and all these things will be given to you as well" (Matt. 6:33). This advice is important not only for those who might be preoccupied with the question of marriage in an unhealthy way, but for all of us.

I would never expect any person to give up marriage like the Apostle Paul did; the call to celibacy must be felt from within. But unless marriage is God's will (and this is often difficult to discern), every one of us should be willing to give it up (Phil. 3:8). When the light of Jesus breaks into our life, we will find strength to surrender to him so radically that everything will find its true proportion.

Contrary to the widely accepted belief that the healthiest relationship is the most private one, I have come to see that engagement and marriage are concerns of the whole church, not just of the individuals involved. Therefore, when young men and women in my church feel drawn to one another, I advise them to turn first to their parents, and then to a pastor. From this moment on their relationship is placed under the care of the church. Our young people do not regard this step as an imposition, nor do they feel they are being chaperoned. On the contrary, they are grateful for the possibility of guidance in an area where immaturity and impurity bring misery to many.

Naturally, this approach will only work in a congregation ruled by love and trust, and every couple must decide how it applies to their situation. For some, it may be hard to understand the purpose of seeking guidance. Others may shy away from the idea completely. Yet the simple lesson of opening up to people one trusts deserves serious attention.

Ray and his fiancée, Helen, met at our church a few years ago. Below, Ray shares their story:

Saturday nights, when I wasn't working late at Armani Exchange, I'd go clubbing with a handful of friends. Or maybe head for Third Street in Santa Monica, or just drive down to the pier and hang out. The scene rarely changed. Only the girls. Nothing serious, never anything "going on" – just someone to split the tab on a few rounds or hit the dance floor with. Sometimes I'd meet someone I thought was special, someone I wanted to see more of. We'd trade numbers, and maybe arrange for the dinner-and-movie thing. It was all so harmless, so effortless.

At least that's how I viewed it then, nearly three years ago, before I got to know Helen.

Both of us grew up in the same church. We met as teenagers, but though we both had feelings for each other, we did not disclose these. After high school, we moved apart. She headed for college, and landed a teaching job; I left for "the world." But after a six-month stint as a volunteer overseas, a couple semesters of college on the East Coast, and a year spent running around Southern California, the nagging sensation that my life was a farce finally cornered me. I had to admit what I had tried to deny for so long – that an intense emptiness and listlessness was masquerading behind my party-hard attitude. My lifestyle did nothing to satisfy my desire for wholeness. My encounters with others, particularly with women, were at best superficial. Often, they were damaging.

For the first time in my life I realized how much I needed the healing power that Christ alone can give. I knew I could not find this on my own, that I needed the support of others I could trust, so I returned home to my parents. Convinced that I wanted God to be the center of my life, I committed my life to him and to the members of my church.

By then I'd made my parents and my pastor aware of my feelings for Helen, and they advised me to let things develop naturally, in God's time: "If your relationship is God's will, it will happen, and no one will be able to stand in the way of it." But they encouraged me to go ahead and talk with her.

I did. It didn't take long for us to realize that something was happening between us. Neither of us would have dared call it love at the time – it was too new, too precious. But as weeks became months, we felt a deep connection growing between us. We spent time together, sometimes with each other's families,

sometimes on our own. We would mull over issues
of faith, read from the Bible, pray, or just sit quietly
together. Later, when my job necessitated a move, we
wrote to each other almost every day.

As our friendship deepened, our openness grew. But
trust, we learned, takes time. At first, it was something
of a revelation to realize that we both had shortcomings.
We could hurt each other, and at times even betray the
love taking shape between us. Yet whenever we became
entrenched in our own narrowness, our parents and
pastors were there to help guide us through.

Of course, opening up to someone was sometimes
painful, even embarrassing – especially when things
weren't going smoothly. And the advice our parents or
other church members would give didn't always sit well
with us. But once we discovered the incredible value of
having trusted people to confide in, we realized we were
being granted an opportunity for our relationship to
unfold within a supportive environment.

Now, as our wedding nears, we are grateful for
the help of others who have steered us toward Christ.
Without them, Helen and I would most likely never
have found each other's hearts. In our era, we know
what a rare gift it is that our relationship has been able
to deepen without the pressures caused by revolving
around sex. And we know that no matter what our
future brings, Christ will remain our guide.

Ray and Helen's story illustrates how vitally important
it is for a couple to take plenty of time to get to know
each other inwardly before making any commitment.
When two people seek marriage, it is essential that
they first strive to discover all there is of God in each
other. There are plenty of wholesome activities a couple

can find for this purpose: reading, hiking, visiting each other's families, or participating in a community service project together. Writing to each other is also a good way to become acquainted on a deeper level. In my experience, it is best if such correspondence starts out in a non-binding way – as if from a brother to his sister and vice versa. This is because emotional appeals about romantic love and belonging together, far from providing a foundation for the future, do the opposite: they obscure the clarity needed to discern whether or not a future commitment is really God's will.

My church encourages young couples not only to correspond, but also to share what they have written with either a parent or pastor. Such openness may seem extreme, but it allows for support and guidance. One can only wonder how many marriages might be saved if young couples everywhere had the humility to turn to their parents (or any other married couple they trust) for advice, even if not in this specific way.

Again, a healthy relationship cannot be rushed. Like a flower, it must be allowed to open in God's time, not forced in hopes of an early bloom. If a marriage is to last, it must be built on a carefully laid foundation.

What matters most, in the decision to marry, is God's will.

Honesty is fundamental to every healthy relationship. If a couple does not feel that they are growing closer to each other and to God, they must be open about it. Here the church, too, must care enough about its members to be honest with them – to help a couple discern if they are really meant for one another, and to consider whether their friendship is bearing good fruit. Even if no promise has been made, ending a relationship is painful. But better a painful end than the endless pain of a relationship that leads nowhere.

Only when two young people, independently of each other and with the input of their parents and minister, feel assured over a period of time that they really belong together for life are they ready to become engaged. Only when they feel in the depths of their hearts that this is the person meant for them, and that it is God alone who has led them together, are they truly ready to make a bond for life.

Once engaged, most couples want to participate fully in their love and express it actively in giving and receiving. Their hearts are set on making each other as happy and fulfilled as possible, and they feel ready to do anything to bring this about. All the more, such couples must realize that the powers of love are much greater than they themselves, and they must ask God daily for the strength to discipline themselves.

Long embraces, caressing, mouth-to-mouth kissing, and anything else that might lead to sexual arousal should be avoided. The desire for physical closeness is natural, but instead of revolving around this desire, an engaged couple should focus on getting to know each other more intimately on a deeper level and nurturing each other's love to Jesus and the church.

When two people are getting to know each other, sexual involvement inhibits the development of a well-founded relationship. As soon as sex is on stage, it steals the show. Sexual excitement is progressive in its nature: once you begin you are never satisfied in going back. When two people intentionally arouse each other, they are engaging in a form of foreplay. Whether they acknowledge it or not, they are preparing themselves emotionally and physically for intercourse. They are left with only two choices: to go all the way, or to stop short and experience the emotional frustration of being aroused and not satisfied. The desires kindled within them cannot be appeased without sinning. "Going halfway" is therefore harmful, because it interferes with building lasting intimacy.

A marriage that starts with a conscience burdened by unconfessed sin is a marriage without a stable foundation, and it can be set right only through confession and repentance. The health of a marriage depends on the ground in which it grows. If it is sown in the soil of purity and faith, it will bear good fruit and have God's blessing.

Try to grasp the spirit, not the letter, of what I have written. If you are considering marriage, seek to understand each other's inmost heart, and turn to Christ in trust to find his answer to every question. He will never fail to lead you clearly.

14

The Service of Singleness

The disciples said to him, "If this is the situation between a husband and wife, it is better not to marry." Jesus replied, "Not everyone can accept this word, but only those to whom it has been given. For there are eunuchs who were born that way, and there are eunuchs who have been made eunuchs by others – and there are those who choose to live like eunuchs for the sake for the kingdom of heaven. The one who can accept this should accept it."

Matthew 19:10–12

THE GIFT OF UNITY, whether with other people or with God, does not depend in any way on marriage. In fact, the New Testament teaches that a deeper dedication to Christ may be found by giving up marriage for the sake of the kingdom of God. Those who renounce everything for Jesus, including the gift of marriage, are given a great promise by him: he will be especially near to them at his return (Rev. 14:1–5). Whether such people find themselves without a life partner because of abandonment, death, or lack of opportunity, they can find a much greater calling than marriage if they are able to accept their singleness in the depths of their hearts. They can dedicate their lives in a special way to undivided service for God's kingdom.

To live fully is to live for Christ.

Every man and every woman on earth who desires to follow Christ must be completely transformed by him. This challenge takes on a deeper meaning for those who are single (for whatever reason) and who carry their singleness for Christ's sake. Such a person will find a special relationship to him.

A life lived for Christ is life in its fullest sense (John 10:10). We must never forget this; it is our deepest calling. If we truly love Christ the Bridegroom with undivided hearts, we will be immersed in him just as we are immersed in water at baptism. If we live in Christ, our love for him will guide our love to our Christian brothers and sisters and to all those around us.

The story of Saint Francis of Assisi and his friendship with Saint Clare shows in a wonderful way the significance of brotherly and sisterly love – even when it does not lead to marriage. When all of Francis's brothers and friends deserted him, he went to Clare. In her he had a friend he could rely on. Even after his death she remained loyal to him and continued to carry out his mission, despite opposition. Here was a relationship that had nothing to do with marriage but was still genuinely intimate – a friendship of true purity and unity in God.

There will always be women and men like Clare and Francis who remain unmarried for the sake of Christ. Yet we must recognize that the gift of a relationship such as theirs is not given to everyone. In struggling for purity, most single people are no different from married people. Even a life committed to celibacy is no safeguard against impurity – in every heart, purity requires constant watchfulness, a daily fight against the flesh, and a firm attitude against sin.

If we allow him, Jesus can fill every void.
The Scriptures never promise us the removal of temptation. But we do have the assurance that it need not overcome us (1 Cor. 10:13). If we prove ourselves in patience and faithfulness, God will help us. This is not to say that it is possible to keep pure by the strength of our own will. Yet by the power of the Holy Spirit, and through the help of caring friends and family members, it is possible to find freedom and victory (Gal. 6:1–2).

For those who do not find a partner in marriage but feel no special calling to remain single for the sake of Jesus, there is a danger of bitterness. If a deep yearning for marriage remains unfulfilled, especially over a long period of time, it can harden the heart. Then only God's grace can protect the soul and enable it to let go – to give up marriage and still find peace.

Cynthia, an unmarried woman in her mid-forties, offers her insights on how to avoid an empty life and find lasting fulfillment:

"Me, single for the rest of my life?" Many of us must face this reality. Why? – because we have chosen to commit our lives to God first. He needs tools that are unattached to family to serve him. Does this mean less fulfillment, stunted growth, withdrawal from full involvement in life? Not if one can embrace, instead of rebel against, God's plan for one's life. In fact, a dedicated life of service awaits those who sacrifice or renounce marriage in order to keep themselves completely at God's disposal.

Think of single people like the writer Amy Carmichael, who traveled to India as a young missionary, not knowing what kind of service God wanted of her.

She soon had a growing orphanage of children rescued from virtual slavery in the clutches of the Hindu temple priests. Or think of Mother Teresa, who founded an order of sisters to look after the poorest of the poor in Calcutta. Her order has spread all over the world. Or think of Paul and others of the apostles who, because they were single, were able to travel ceaselessly to spread the Gospel.

Of course you don't have to be a missionary, nun, or apostle to find fulfillment in a life of singleness. I could have felt bitterness and frustration at not being married, but instead I have found plenty of opportunities to serve others on a daily basis right where I have been placed.

Almost weekly I visit inmates at the local jail. During my last visit, the women in the jail were eager for Bible study, so we read the story of the Good Samaritan and talked about its everyday applications. After a discussion of who could or couldn't sing, we all joined in singing spirituals and hymns like "Precious Lord" and "Amazing Grace."

Needless to say, not every evening is satisfying in this way. Loneliness can be a reality in any single person's life. It may tempt one to self-pity, but like any temptation, it can be refused. In her book *Passion and Purity,* Elisabeth Elliot advises: "Accept your loneliness. It is one stage, and only one stage, on a journey that brings you to God. It will not always last. Offer up your loneliness to God, as the little boy offered to Jesus his five loaves and two fishes. God can transform it for the good of others. Above all, do something for somebody else!"

Here is the clue: service rendered to others. Teaching, nursing, counseling, or visiting prisoners in jail – any of such activities can lead to a fulfilled life. For there are many hurting people in the world who need an extra touch of love, and those of us who are single are uniquely free to take up the task of being there for them.

The process of letting go of one's own desires is never easy, and it may at times weigh very heavily on a person. But when single people are able to surrender their own hopes and dreams completely, Jesus will fill the void that might otherwise burden them. They will remember how he ended his life on the cross, and they will find joy in bearing singleness as their sacrifice for him. Those who continually long for marriage, despite the fact that God has not given it to them, can never attain this joy. Marriage is a great gift, but to belong completely and undividedly to Christ is a greater gift.

Ultimately, we have to be willing to be used by God as he wills and find contentment in whatever circumstances we find ourselves (Phil. 4:11–13). We should never think that God does not love us. Such a thought is of the devil.

Naturally, no matter how dedicated a single person is, he or she will still experience moments, days, or even weeks of sadness and struggle. The knowledge that marriage and children are beyond reach will always bring pangs of longing and a sense of loss. But rather than dwell on these things, it is better (even if harder) to look to God and to turn to one's brothers and sisters in the church. Bonhoeffer writes:

> Pain is a holy angel who shows us treasures that would otherwise remain forever hidden; through him men and women have become greater than through all the joys of the world. It must be so and I tell myself this in my present situation over and over again. The pain of suffering and of longing, which can often be felt even physically, must be there, and we cannot and need not

talk it away. But it needs to be overcome every time, and thus there is an even holier angel than the one of pain; that is, the one of joy in God.²⁴

*Singleness can be accepted as a burden –
or as a special calling.*

Single men and women must not fall into the trap of estranging themselves from life and love in bitterness. They must not stifle what is best in themselves or give themselves over to dreams or to desires that cannot be satisfied. They must not let self-circling fantasies block the unfolding of all that God has given them. If they are able to accept their singleness as a gift or a special calling, they will let none of their energy or love go unused. Their longings will be fulfilled in giving: in a stream of love that moves away from themselves, and toward Christ and the church. As Paul says:

> An unmarried man is concerned about the Lord's affairs – how he can please the Lord. But a married man is concerned about the affairs of this world – how he can please his wife – and his interests are divided. An unmarried woman or virgin is concerned about the Lord's affairs: her aim is to be devoted to the Lord in both body and spirit. But a married woman is concerned about the affairs of this world – how she can please her husband. I am saying this for your own good, not to restrict you, but that you may live in a right way in undivided devotion to the Lord (1 Cor. 7:32–35).

Earlier in the same letter, Paul refers to another blessing of singleness: the lack of care and worry over spouse and children, especially in times of hardship. "Those who marry will face many troubles in this life, and I want to spare you this" (1 Cor. 7:28).

Widows, like the unmarried, are also able to serve the church and the needy at times when a married person could not. Paul says, "A woman who is really widowed and left without anybody can give herself up to God in hope and consecrate all her days and nights to petitions and meetings for prayer" (1 Tim. 5:5 Jerusalem Bible). In the early church in Jerusalem, widows were appointed to serve the poor or entrusted with other responsibilities. "Even in the smallest church community, the overseer had to be a friend of the poor, and there was at least one widow responsible to see to it, day and night, that no sick or needy person was neglected."[25]

How sad it is that today it is very often the widows – and other single women and men – who are themselves neglected and lonely! May the church always be ready to meet the needs of such people (1 Cor. 12:26). Especially with the collapse of the family, we must find new ways to show single members extra love and care and to involve them in the lives of our families or fellowships. This does not mean pressing them to find a spouse and then pitying them if they don't – that will only add to their pain. It means welcoming their gifts and services in the church, providing them with meaningful tasks, and drawing them into the inner life of the church so that they may find fulfillment.

No matter our state, all of us are called to love.
Those of us who are married should recognize that our happiness is a gift – something to be shared and passed on. We should reach out to those who struggle with feelings

of loneliness. This is why in my congregation every single person is "adopted" into some family. Here they can give as well as receive. Most important, all of us, whether married or single, should remember that true fulfillment and joy is found in serving one another in the spirit of community. We are called to a love that gives unconditionally – not to the grasping love of a cozy marriage nor to the indulging love of isolated self-pity.

As Christians, we know that true love is found in its most perfect form in Jesus. Many of us have been touched by Jesus, or been called and used by him. But that is not enough. Each of us must ask God to let us experience him personally – in the very depths of our hearts. Our eyes must be fixed on him and him alone so that we can see him as he really is, and not grow weary and lose heart (Heb. 12:2–3).

The span of life is short, and as Paul warns us, the world in its present form is passing away (1 Cor. 7:29–31). What we need most in our time is Christ, but not only as a guide or an image before our eyes. He must become a living reality in our daily lives. He said, "I have come to bring fire on the earth, and how I wish it were already kindled!" (Luke 12:49).

Where is Christ most clearly revealed as he was and still is? We must seek for him with our brothers and sisters. We must ask that he is revealed today and every day among us. More than that, we must ask for the courage to witness to him before others just as he is, with tenderness, meekness, and humility, but also in truth, clarity, and sharpness. We must not add or take away anything from his gospel. That is the essence of single-heartedness, and the service of singleness.

The Spirit of our Age

15

With or Without God

Follow God's example, therefore, as dearly loved
children, and walk in the way of love, just as Christ
loved us and gave himself up for us.....Among you
there must not be even a hint of sexual immorality,
or of any kind of impurity, or of greed, because these
are improper for God's holy people. Nor should
there be obscenity, foolish talk or coarse joking....
Let no one deceive you with empty words, for
because of such things God's wrath comes on those
who are disobedient.

Ephesians 5:1–6

THROUGHOUT SCRIPTURE the covenant of God
with his people and the unity of Christ with his church
is compared to the union of marriage. In our culture,
however, marriage – the very thing we should honor and
celebrate most as love – has been attacked, dragged into
the dirt, and destroyed by the spirits of impurity and
irreverence.

For many people today, love is a delusion.
The desecration of love is one of the greatest tragedies
of our time. Increasingly, love is understood as nothing
more than desire, and the satisfaction of this desire is seen

as fulfillment. People talk about sexual liberation but remain trapped in bondage to their sexual desires; they talk about true love but live in self-absorbed estrangement. Our age is a loveless age: relationships and hearts are broken everywhere, millions of human lives are discarded almost before they have begun, thousands of children are abused or abandoned, and fear and mistrust abound even in supposedly healthy marriages. Love has been reduced to sex. Because of this, it is nothing more than a delusion for many – short-lived intimacy followed by gnawing emptiness and anguish.

How can we rediscover the real meaning of love? So many things in the world today take away our belief in lasting and unconditional love. So much of what is called "love" these days really has to do with the excitement and passion of lust. We live in a sex-obsessed, sex-crazed society, and everything reeks of it – advertising, literature, fashion, and entertainment. Marriage has been the first casualty: its significance has become so distorted that its true meaning has been lost.

Of course, no honest person can lay the blame for all of this at the door of the media or of some vague force in society. Certainly, the media has confused thousands of people and left them hardened. And political agendas to redefine marriage altogether, in civil law and even in churches, have deepened this confusion in powerfully destructive ways. But it is we – each one of us – whose souls are burdened by the sin of our own lust, whose marriages have fallen apart, whose children have gone astray. We cannot ignore our own misdeeds; we must take responsibility for our own actions, for every instance where we have accepted the spirit of impurity and let evil into our own hearts. We have mocked and twisted the image of God and separated ourselves from our creator. We must learn to listen again to the deepest cries of our hearts, and repent and turn back to God.

Fifty years have passed since the beginning of the sexual revolution, and its devastating aftermath should be obvious to anyone: widespread promiscuity; teen pregnancy and suicide; tens of millions of abortions; the spread of sexually transmitted diseases; child pornography; the erosion of the family and home life; and generations of fatherless children. "We have sown the wind, and reap the whirlwind" (Hos. 8:7).

Our time grossly overestimates the importance of sex. Whether on bookstands, at supermarket counters, or on the screen, its significance is exaggerated in a thoroughly unhealthy way. Love between man and woman is no longer regarded as sacred or noble; it has become a commodity seen only in an animal sense, as an uncontrollable impulse that must be satisfied.

As a tool of the sexual revolution, modern sex education is largely responsible for all this. Sex education was supposed to bring us freedom, enlightened attitudes, responsibility, and safety. Isn't it obvious by now that it has been a failure? Haven't we seen by now that knowledge is no safeguard, and that sex education as taught in most schools has only increased sexual activity?

True education for the sexual life instills reverence.

Most parents have very little, if any, idea of what their children are taught in sex education classes. Sex education has never been a simple presentation of biological facts. In many curricula students are graphically taught (sometimes by way of films) about various sexual practices, including masturbation, and about "safe" sex. In others, sexual perversions are openly and explicitly discussed and presented as normal ways of finding sexual "fulfillment." In some school districts an appreciation and understanding for bisexual and homosexual lifestyles are encouraged: they are, our children are told, perfectly acceptable alternatives to heterosexual marriage. Some schools even have students pair off to discuss topics such as foreplay and orgasm. Antibiotics and abortion are presented as positive safety nets in case contraception and "safe" sex practices fail. Abstinence, if not entirely ignored, is mentioned only in passing. As William Bennett, former Secretary of Education, writes:

> There is a coarseness, a callousness, a cynicism, a banality, and a vulgarity to our time. There are too many signs of a civilization gone rotten. And the worst of it has to do with our children: we live in a culture that at times seems almost dedicated to the corruption of the young, to ensuring the loss of their innocence before their time.[26]

Sex education is little more than "safe" sex training. Initially, it was instituted as an attempt to bank the fires of teenage sexuality; instead, it has only fanned the flames.[27] Most people seem to take it for granted that teenagers will and should express themselves sexually. But again, the result has been millions of abortions, countless unwed mothers on public support, and an epidemic of sexually transmitted diseases. Clearly, the idea that accurate knowledge fosters responsible behavior is nothing less than a grand myth.

In general, much of what is taught today in the name of sex education is a horror, and as Christians we must protest against it. It is often little more than the formalized training of irreverence, impurity, and rebellion against the plan of God.

True education for the sexual life takes place best between parent and child in an environment of reverence and trust. To educate anyone about sex through anonymous images and impersonal information will only awaken the sexual impulse of a child prematurely and, in his mind, separate sex from love and commitment.

Obviously we should not be afraid to talk freely with our own children about sexual matters, especially as they approach adolescence. Otherwise they will learn about these things first from their peers or the internet, and rarely in a reverent atmosphere. All the same, there is a danger in giving a child too many biological facts about sex. Often, a factual approach to sex robs it of its divine mystery.

To the Christian parent, sex education means guiding the sexual conscience of his or her children to sense their own dignity and the dignity of others. It means helping them to understand that selfish pleasure, whether it "hurts" anybody else or not, is contrary to love (Gal. 5:13). It means teaching them that, separated from God, sexual intercourse or any other sexual activity burdens the conscience and undermines honest relationships. It means opening their eyes to see the deep emptiness that leads people – and could lead them too – into sexual sin.

A child can acquire a healthy attitude to his body and to sex quite naturally, simply by being taught that his body, as the temple of the Spirit, is holy, and that any defilement of it is sin. I will never forget the deep impression it made on me as a young teen when my father took me for a walk and told me about the struggle for a pure life and the importance of keeping myself pure for the woman I might find and marry someday. He said to me, "If you are able to live a pure life now, it will be easier for the rest of your life. But if you give in now to personal impurity, it will become harder and harder to withstand temptation, even once you marry."

Parents who want to protect their children from impurity should remember that the discipline of work – whether through chores, exercise, or through other activities – is one of the best safeguards. Children who have been taught to stick to a task and see it through will be better equipped to deal with sexual temptations than children who have been pampered and catered to.

Any misuse of sex cuts us off
from our true selves and from each other.

Young people underestimate the power of the demonic forces they allow into their lives when they give in to impurity. Take masturbation, for example. As children grow into young men and women, their sexual desire increases, and often their most immediate impulse is to seek sexual gratification through masturbation. Today many parents, educators, and ministers claim that masturbation is healthy and natural; they see it as just another form of stress release. And the sexual fantasy and activity it often leads to, even among children who have barely reached puberty, is considered by some to be normal.

Why are we parents and educators so afraid to speak the truth – to warn our children not only of the dangers of promiscuity but also of masturbation? (Prov. 5:1 ff.) Aren't both illnesses of the soul? Don't both desecrate and betray the image of God, and undermine the marriage bond? Masturbation can never bring true satisfaction. It is a solitary act. It is self-stimulation, self-gratification, self-abuse – it closes us within a dream world and separates us from genuine relationships. When it becomes habitual (which it often does), it aggravates isolation and loneliness, and it intensifies feelings of futility and frustration. At its worst, as a breach in the bond of unity and love for which sex is created, it is comparable to adultery. I have counseled many young people who are enslaved by masturbation: they earnestly desire to be freed from their habit, but they fall into it again and again.

A person who struggles with masturbation is often too ashamed to talk about it with anyone. Yet it is important to realize that because shameful acts work in secrecy, their power can only be broken when they are brought to light. Certainly sharing one's burdens and inner feelings with a mentor or pastor can be painful, but this is the only recourse for anyone who wants to become truly free.

People may struggle with masturbation right to the end of their lives. I have counseled men in their eighties who still have not found freedom from it. The question arises whether there is anything one can do to be rid of this curse. My advice to those enslaved to masturbation is to seek strength through prayer. You will not conquer your addiction by will power alone. Before you go to bed at night, turn your thoughts to God and read something of an inner, spiritual nature. Even then the temptation to masturbate can arise. When that happens, find something to take your mind off it – get out of bed and take a walk, or do some household chore. Often a simple activity provides the best means to overcome these strong temptations.

Frequently enslavement to masturbation is connected to another form of bondage: pornography. Very few people will admit an addiction to pornography, but the fact that it is a billion-dollar industry shows how widespread it is, also among "Christians."

Many people claim that pornography should not be criminalized because it is "victimless." Yet anything that encourages impurity, even in the form of solitary sexual arousal, is a crime because it degrades the human body, which was created in God's image as a temple of the soul (1 Cor. 6:19). The so-called lines typically drawn between pornography, masturbation, one-night stands, and prostitution are actually an illusion. All of them are means used to attain sexual satisfaction without the "burden" of commitment. All reduce the mystery of sex to a technique for satisfying lust. And all of them are shameful – the secrecy of those who indulge in them betrays that fact more clearly than anything else (Rom. 13:12–13).

Prayer and confession can free us
from the burden of impurity.

No one can free himself from impurity or any other sin in his own strength. Freedom comes through the attitude of inner poverty, through continually turning to God.

The struggle against temptation is in everyone and will always be there, but through prayer and confession, sin can be overcome.

Whenever we let down our guard in the struggle for purity – whenever we allow passion and lust to overcome us – we are in danger of throwing ourselves completely away. Then we will not be able to drive away the evil spirits we have allowed to enter, and the intervention of Christ himself will be needed to bring freedom. Without this, there will be only deepening hopelessness and despair.

In the most extreme instances the desperation brought on by a secret life of impurity ends in suicide. This can only be described as a rebellion against God, a statement that says, "I'm beyond hope – my problems are too big even for God to handle." Suicide denies that God's grace is greater than our weakness. If we find ourselves in the abyss of despair, the only answer is to seek God and ask for his compassion and mercy. Even when we find ourselves at the end of our rope, God wants to give us new hope and courage, no matter how deeply we feel we have betrayed him. God is always ready to forgive every sin (1 John 1:9); we only need to be humble enough to ask him. When someone is tempted by thoughts of suicide, the most important thing we can do is to show him love – to remind him that each of us was created by and for God, and that each of us has a purpose to fulfill.

To turn from sin and to realize that we are created for God is always a revelation and a joy. If we faithfully live before God in our lifetime here on earth, we will recognize the magnitude of our wonderful task, the task of receiving his love and sharing it with others. There is no calling more wonderful.

16

What about Homosexuality?

*For you were once darkness, but now you are light
in the Lord. Live as children of light (for the fruit of
the light consists in all goodness, righteousness and
truth) and find out what pleases the Lord. Have
nothing to do with the fruitless deeds of darkness,
but rather expose them. For it is shameful even to
mention what the disobedient do in secret.*

Ephesians 5:8–12

WHEN, BACK IN 1995, a panel of the Church of
England recommended that the phrase "living in sin"
be abandoned and that unmarried couples, heterosexual
and homosexual alike, be "given encouragement and
support" in their lifestyles, most Christians were alarmed.
Suggesting that "loving homosexual relations and acts"
are intrinsically no less valuable than heterosexual ones,
the panel proposed that love should be allowed to be
expressed "in a variety of relationships."[28] Today such
a statement would hardly raise eyebrows; dozens of
denominations have asserted similar ideas, and people
who disagree are hesitant to speak out. In the name of
"tolerance" and "openness," Christ's teachings have been
replaced by a false gospel that insists that sinful behavior
is normal, even blessed by God.

Same-sex "marriage" was a fringe idea far out of the mainstream at the time of the Church of England panel's report. Today it is the law of the land in much of the western world and beyond. Many politicians and an increasing number of clergy and ordinary people are afraid to say anything against this movement for fear of losing friends or their position. Very few dare to stand in opposition and say, "Enough!" But by refusing to recognize marriage as a covenant between one man and one woman, they not only call into question the entire institution of the family, but flatly deny God's order of creation. They are sending children the wrong message: that anything is okay as long as two people have feelings of love for one another, and that life-long commitment to one person of the opposite sex is merely one of many options.

All the more, those of us who believe in God's unchanging truths must not be afraid to witness to his wonderful plan for human sexuality, and to demonstrate the beauty and freedom of a life of purity.

We must love everyone – and that is why we must also speak out against sin.

Every one of us is a sinner and falls short every day. Homosexual acts are no worse than other sins, and we know from the Bible that no transgression is so terrible that it cannot be forgiven or healed (Eph. 2:3–5). To mistreat gays or to judge a practicing homosexual more harshly than any other person is wrong.

The saying "Hate the sin but love the sinner" has been derided by gay-rights advocates, but in reality it expresses a fundamental truth of the gospel that applies to all people, not just those struggling with homosexual inclinations. Jesus came to set all of us free from sin. It's true that he accepts each one of us, yet he loves us too much to allow us to remain as we are. He hates the evil that enslaves us, and gave up his life to redeem us from it.

To affirm homosexual relationships is to deny God's creative intent.

Homosexual conduct is a sin. It is "against nature," against God's creative design, and it is a form of self-worship and idolatry (Rom. 1:26). As a sexual act between two people of the same gender it is the "very grievous" sin of Sodom and Gomorrah (Gen. 18:20).

In Leviticus 18:22–23, God calls homosexual intercourse an abomination: "Do not have sexual relations with a man as one does with a woman; that is detestable." Let those who discount this prohibition by arguing that we are now "no longer under the law, but under grace" then explain why the prohibitions on incest, adultery, bestiality, and human sacrifice are not to be likewise ignored. All of these abominations are condemned in the very next sentences of the same passage.

The New Testament also condemns homosexual behavior. In Romans 1:26–28 Paul writes:

> Even their women exchanged natural sexual relations for unnatural ones. In the same way the men also abandoned natural relations with women and were inflamed with lust for one another. Men committed shameful acts with other men, and received in themselves the due penalty for their error.

And in 1 Cor. 6:9–10 Paul writes:

> Or do you not know that wrongdoers will not inherit the kingdom of God? Do not be deceived: Neither the sexually immoral nor idolaters nor adulterers nor men who have sex with men . . . will inherit the kingdom of God.

Many people reinterpret these Scriptures as condemning only offensive homosexual (and heterosexual) behavior. But isn't it clear that when Paul speaks of "homosexual offenders" he is speaking of the offense of homosexual behavior itself? If only "offensive" kinds of homosexual acts were evil, then what about the rest of what Paul mentions in the same passage: adultery, idolatry, and so forth?

What could be clearer than Paul's words in Romans, where he calls homosexual conduct "sinful desire, sexual impurity" and says that it is "degrading and shameful"? Or his unmistakably sharp words against giving oneself over "to a depraved mind"? (Rom. 1:24–28) Homosexual acts are always wrong, for they always distort God's will for creation. They simply cannot be defended in any way by Scripture.[29] And this is just as true when they take place in a "loving" lifelong relationship. Adulterous heterosexual affairs may also be felt to be loving and may be long-lasting, but that doesn't make them right.

It is typical today to hear people talk about the injustice of holding homosexuals responsible for an orientation that they themselves did not necessarily choose. But this misses the point. Whether or not homosexuals are responsible for their sexual orientation has no relevance as to the rightness or wrongness of their behavior. To explain behavior is one thing. To justify it is altogether different.

A spate of books has recently been published arguing that the Bible never condemns same-sex "marriage"; it only rejects certain kinds of homosexual behavior: rape, ritual prostitution, and promiscuous sex. They argue that nowhere does it condemn homosexual attraction, per se, nor committed relationships between two consenting adults of the same sex.[30] But what these books fail to remember is God's original purpose for sex and his original plan for marriage: the joining together of a man and a woman who become "one flesh" to make possible the creation of a new life. In other words, sexual love as God intended it is far more than an intense feeling of mutual attraction or a sexual-romantic partnership. If that is all marriage means, then open marriages, incestuous relationships, or polyamorous relationships including multiple partners would also have to be affirmed. After all, such relationships may also be "loving" and long-lasting. But clearly even where this is the case, that doesn't make such relationships right, or biblical.[31]

Whatever its origin or kind,
sexual temptation can be overcome.

The sexual desires of a homosexual can be acute, but so can those of anyone else. All of us are "naturally" predisposed to do what we should not do. But if we believe in God, we must also believe that he can give us the grace to overcome whatever struggles we may have to bear: "My grace is sufficient for you, for my power is made perfect in weakness" (2 Cor. 12:9–10).

In speaking out against such sins, we must always remember that even though scripture condemns homosexual behavior, it never gives us license to condemn those who engage in it. As Christians we certainly cannot condone the denial of any person's basic human rights, for whatever reason. It is all too easy to forget that the Bible has much more to say about pride, greed, resentment, and self-righteousness than about homosexuality.

Nevertheless, we need to resist the agenda of those who try to present homosexuality as just another lifestyle – especially as it affects the legalization of same-sex "marriages" – as well as efforts to compel religious groups to go against their basic beliefs and accept practicing homosexuals as members and even ministers.

It is also important to consider the difference between homosexual inclinations or orientation and an active homosexual lifestyle. Whereas homosexual orientation can arise by means of psychological influences, social environment, and perhaps genetic makeup, an active homosexual lifestyle is a matter of choice. To argue that our culture, family, development, or genes make us powerless to choose for or against sin is to deny the concept of free will.

As an orientation, homosexuality is an especially deep-rooted condition, and those who struggle with it deserve compassion and help. Therefore we always need to be ready to receive the homosexual man or woman into our fellowship and stand with him or her – in patience and love, though also with the clarity that refuses to tolerate continued sinning. Above all, we need to remind those burdened with same-sex attraction that they are more than their sexuality.

I have counseled many people who have struggled with homosexual temptations. Sometimes a person's situation seems hopeless, but in my experience, even someone who has been ingrained in the gay lifestyle for a long time can be helped. Whether a struggling person acts on his temptations or not, one thing remains the same: if he turns single-mindedly to Jesus, he can be helped and freed; if he is divided in the depths of his heart, even the most valiant efforts to resist temptation will cramp him spiritually. Even a perverse glance shows that a person is not decided – and Jesus calls this "adultery" in the heart. Lasting freedom can be found only in decisiveness.

It is all the more important, therefore, that people who are not burdened by homosexuality try to understand the tremendous inner need, pain, and loneliness with which homosexuals live.[32] Their misplaced sexual desire often stems from an intense yearning for a genuinely loving connection with others. Many homosexuals have never known unconditional, accepting love from those of their own gender. In fatherless and abusive homes across our country, a void exists that is capable of inducing homosexual feelings in children. And in our culture, driven as it is by competition and the will to dominate, it is easy for some people to feel left out; they may turn to homosexual activity as a result.

I have known Howard and his wife, Ann, ever since they joined our church two decades ago, yet it was not until recently that I fully understood the depth of Howard's struggle. Abused as a child by his uncle, neglected by his workaholic father, and ridiculed by his peers for his lack of athletic ability, Howard grew up feeling misunderstood and out of place. He craved attention: from his father, other men, and boys his own age. By the time he was in his mid-teens, he was homosexually active. While Howard does not blame his upbringing for choices he made later in life, his story should warn every parent of what can happen when children grow up without the support of a caring family.

But Howard's story is more than a warning. It bears witness to Christ's power to redeem; to the importance of repentance; to the healing force of forgiveness; and to the joy that every one of us can know. He writes:

> When I was sixteen, I began to mess around with other boys. It wasn't long before I allowed older men to "experiment" with me. These sexual experiences excited me, but they left me feeling very guilty. I was not able to open up to anyone about what I was going through. I even lied to my father when he confronted me directly and asked if I had such feelings.
>
> By the time I turned twenty-one, I had done virtually every homosexual act possible. Nothing satisfied me. My encounters with other men were empty; I preferred to look at pictures and create my own fantasies. I never tried to come to terms with my attraction to men, excusing it as something I "couldn't help." Even when my insurance paid for psychotherapy because of work-related stress and anxiety, I did not tell the psychiatrist anything personal. I was convinced: there was no point talking to anyone; no one would understand me, and it wasn't possible for me to change, anyway.
>
> I married the first woman I had a sexual relationship with. Ann loved me and accepted what she knew of me. We talked about our personal feelings from the start, but we'd been married two years before I worked up the courage to share my secret with her. Naturally, Ann responded with stunned surprise. She could not understand how it was possible. I told her about my childhood

and about the thoughts and desires that burdened me. I made it clear to her that I wanted nothing to do with these things, and she accepted this and seemed to have hope that I could change. Even though I fell into casual encounters with other men on several more occasions, she continually forgave me.

Many homosexuals were "coming out of the closet" at that time, revealing their lifestyle to family and friends and trying to find acceptance. I dreaded this, because I was sure I would not be accepted. Actually, at heart I did not want acceptance; I wanted help to overcome my problem. Finally I told my story to a lay pastor whom I trusted. He helped me find the strength to share my struggle with a small group of people I knew and felt close to. They were at first shocked, but then also very supportive, knowing that they too had struggles. This was the beginning of my path to recovery. But only the beginning.

Later my wife and I joined an intentional Christian community, sensing that we had arrived at a place where true healing could be found. To a degree this was true, but sometimes when I felt low and depressed, I would still give in to lustful thoughts and looks, which on several occasions nearly led me back into my old ways. Clearly I could never overcome my problems in my own strength. All the same, I kidded myself into believing I could, and convinced my wife I was doing okay. In the meantime, I was blocking out Jesus' words about the lustful look. My conscience became duller and duller. My heart grew harder and harder.

Ann continued to trust me, and God gave us two sons. Yet in spite of these blessings, I sunk deeper and deeper. Then one day a friend discovered me looking at pornography. Though at first I tried to lie my way out, I finally found the courage to admit my sin. I half expected to be "run out of town." But while no one condoned my behavior, I did not feel condemned. Men who I thought would be totally disgusted with me suddenly looked me squarely in the eyes with true, brotherly love. My hard heart began to melt. . . .

My wife and I separated for a while so that I could find my true bearings again. During this time Ann stood faithfully by her commitment to the church community and to me. She told me later, "When we married, I had no idea what we might face in the future. We promised to remain faithful – come hell or high water – to God, to the church, and to each other. We had no idea what we were promising, but I know this is what protected us. This is what led us together again."

Ann was right, of course. It was only through God's grace that I was able to recognize how badly I needed to come completely clean, to open up my heart wider than I ever had before, and to set straight every single wrong act or ingrained attitude from the past. I saw how my own selfishness lay at the root of my problem. Bit by bit, I felt my bondage to darkness breaking.

As my repentance deepened, my heart grew lighter, my mind freer. Finally, I moved back in with my wife and children. Now we are closer as a family than we ever have been. And the curse I have lived with all my life has been transformed into a deep joy. Christ has given me the gift of a clear conscience – there is no greater gift. It gives me courage to face anything that might come in the future. I know I will be tempted for the rest of my life, but I also know that there is always a way through. I can receive help beyond my own strength.

True freedom is possible for every man and woman, and it is up to us to believe this (Gal. 5:1, 13). Howard and Ann's story should remind us not to pretend that victory is easy, or that it can be achieved once and for all. It may not be. For every person who is granted healing, there are dozens more who have to struggle with temptations for years, some for the rest of their lives. Yet is it any different for the rest of us? There cannot be many Christians who have not longed and prayed, seemingly without result, for deliverance from some besetting sin. Ultimately, Christ will free us if we give ourselves unreservedly to him.

For many who experience same-sex attractions, the call to discipleship may mean a celibate single life. Yet the same applies to any Christian who is unable to marry, including the many men and women who long to find a marriage partner but never do. No matter what our situation, whether married or single, we should never doubt that since we are created in God's image, there is always hope for a faithful life of service and love.

17

The Hidden War

Yet you brought me out of the womb; you made
me trust in you, even at my mother's breast. From
birth I was cast upon you; from my mother's womb
you have been my God. Do not be far from me, for
trouble is near and there is no one to help.

Psalm 22:9–11

ALMOST A CENTURY AGO, in response to the idea of "modern" family planning, Eberhard Arnold wrote, "In our families we hope for as many children as God gives. We praise God's creative power and welcome large families as one of his great gifts."[33]

What would he say now, in an era where contraception is standard practice and millions of unborn children are legally murdered every year? Where is our joy in children, and in family life? Our thankfulness for God's gifts? Where is our reverence for life and our compassion for those who are least able to defend themselves? Jesus is very clear that no one can enter the kingdom unless he or she becomes like a child.

Sex without regard for the gift of life is wrong.

The spirit of our age is diametrically opposed not only to the childlike spirit but even to children themselves.[34]

It is a spirit of death, and it can be seen everywhere in modern society: in the rise of murder and suicide rates, in widespread domestic violence, in abortion, the death penalty, and euthanasia. Our culture seems bent on going the way of death, of taking into its own hands what is God's domain. And it is not only the State that is at fault.

How many churches sanction the murder of unborn children under the guise of supporting women's rights? The sexual "liberation" of our society has sowed tremendous destruction. It is a false liberation built on the selfish pursuit of satisfaction and pleasure. It ignores discipline, responsibility, and the real freedom that these can bring. In the words of Stanley Hauerwas, it mirrors "a profound lack of confidence that we have anything worthy to pass on to a new generation. . . . We are willing our deaths."[35]

The majority of people today have no qualms of conscience when the life of a tiny being is prevented or destroyed. Once considered the greatest blessing God can give, children are now considered in terms of their cost: they are a "burden" and a "threat" to the freedom and happiness of the individual.

In a true marriage, there is a close connection between married love and new life (Mal. 2:15). When husband and wife become one flesh, it should always be with the reverent recognition that through it new life may be formed. In this way their sexual union becomes an expression of creative love, a covenant that serves life. But how many couples view sex in this way? For most, the pill has made intercourse a casual act, divorced from responsibility and supposedly free of consequence.

As Christians, we must be willing to speak out against the contraceptive mentality that has infected our society. Too many couples have bought into the popular mindset of sexual indulgence and family planning on demand, throwing to the wind the virtues of self-control and trust. Sex for its own sake, even in marriage, not only cheapens sexual intercourse but erodes the foundation of self-giving love necessary for raising children. To engage in sexual pleasure as an end in itself, without regard for the gift of life, is wrong. It means closing the door to children, and thus despising both the gift and the Giver (Job 1:21). As Mother Teresa once said:

> In destroying the power of giving life, through contraception, a husband or wife is doing something to self. This turns the attention to self, and so it destroys the gift of love in him or her. In loving, the husband and wife must turn the attention to each other, as happens in natural family planning, and not to self, as happens in contraception.[36]

Routine contraception undermines the fulfillment and fruition of two who are one flesh, and because of this we should feel revulsion toward the attitude that consistently seeks to avoid the responsibility of bearing children.

None of this is to suggest that we are to bring children into the world irresponsibly or at the risk of the mother's health and well-being. The size of one's family and the spacing of children is a matter of tremendous responsibility. It is something for each couple to consider before God, with prayer and reverence. Having children too closely together can place an especially difficult burden on the mother. This is an area where a husband has to show loving respect and understanding for his wife. Again, it is vital that a couple turn together to God and place their uncertainties and fears before him in faith (Matt. 7:7–8). If we are open to God's leading, I am confident that he will show us the way.

To abort any child is to mock God.

The contraceptive mentality is but one of the manifestations of the spirit of death that makes new life so unwelcome in so many homes. Everywhere in society today there is a hidden war going on, a war against life. So many little souls are desecrated. And of those who are not prevented by contraception from entering the world, how many are callously destroyed by abortion!

The prevalence of abortion in our society is so great that it makes Herod's slaughter of the Innocents tame in comparison. Abortion is murder – there are no exceptions. If there were, the message of the Gospels would be inconsistent and meaningless. Even the Old Testament makes it clear that God hates the shedding of innocent blood (Prov. 6:16–17). Abortion destroys life and mocks God, in whose image every unborn baby is created.

In the Old Testament there are numerous passages that speak of God's active presence in every human life, even while it is still being formed in the womb. In Genesis 4:1 after Eve conceives and gives birth to Cain, she says, "With the help of the Lord, I have brought forth a man." She does not say, "With the help of Adam," but "with the Lord."

In Psalm 139 we read:

For you created my inmost being; you knit me together in my mother's womb. I praise you because I am fearfully and wonderfully made; your works are wonderful, I know that full well. My frame was not hidden from you when I was made in the secret place. When I was woven together in the depths of the earth, your eyes saw my unformed body. All the days ordained for me were written in your book before one of them came to be (Ps. 139:13–16).

Job exclaims: "Did not he who made me in the womb make them? Did not the same one form us both within our mothers?" (Job 31:15)

And God said to the prophet Jeremiah, "Before I formed you in the womb I knew you, before you were born I set you apart; I appointed you as a prophet to the nations" (Jer. 1:5).

We also read in the New Testament that the unborn are called by God before birth (Gal. 1:15) and that their unique gifts are prophesied while still in the mother's womb. Perhaps one of the most wonderful passages about an unborn child is found in Luke:

When Elizabeth heard Mary's greeting, the baby leaped in her womb, and Elizabeth was filled with the Holy Spirit. In a loud voice she exclaimed: "Blessed are you among women, and blessed is the child you will bear! But why am I so favored, that the mother of my Lord should come to me? As soon as the sound of your greeting reached my ears, the baby in my womb leaped for joy" (Luke 1:41–44).

Here an unborn child, John the Baptist, the forerunner of Jesus, leaped in Elizabeth's womb in acknowledgment of

Jesus, who had been conceived only a short time before. Two unborn children: one capable of responding to the Holy Spirit, and the other – none other than Christ himself – conceived by the Holy Spirit (Matt. 1:20–21).

Clearly, the idea that a new little life comes into being through something merely physical or biological is a complete falsity. It is God who acts in bringing forth life from the womb (Ps. 71:6). Abortion always destroys this act.

This is why the early church universally rejected abortion, and called it infanticide. *The Didache,* the earliest instruction (100 CE) for new Christian converts, leaves no doubt about that: "You shall not slay a child by abortion." And Clement of Alexandria even writes that those who participate in an abortion "wholly lose their own humanity along with the fetus."[37]

Where is the clarity of the church today? Even among so-called Christians, the war of cruelty and death being waged against the innocent unborn children has become a matter of fact, its ghastly horrors and brutal techniques hidden by the mask of medicine and law or even "justified" by every thinkable circumstance.

Who are we to judge whether a life is desirable or not?
I know it is unpopular to say that abortion is murder. I realize that people will say I am removed from reality – that even certain Christian theologians make at least some allowances for abortion. Yet I believe God never does. His law is the law of love. It stands forever, regardless of changing times and changing circumstances: "Thou shalt not kill."

Human life is sacred from conception to death. If we really believe this, we will never be able to accept abortion on any grounds; even the most persuasive arguments about "quality of life" or severe physical deformity or mental retardation will not sway us. Who are we to decide whether or not a little soul should reach the light of day? In God's plan the physically and mentally hindered can be used for God's glory (John 9:1–3). "Who gave human beings their mouths? Who makes them deaf or mute? Who gives them sight or makes them blind? Is it not I, the Lord?" (Exod. 4:11)

How can we dare to judge who is desirable and who is not? The crimes of the Third Reich – where "good" Nordic babies were bred in special nurseries, while retarded babies, children, and adults were sent to gas chambers – should be warning enough. As Dietrich Bonhoeffer writes, "Any distinction between life that is worth living and life that is not worth living must sooner or later destroy life itself."[38]

Even when the life of a pregnant mother is in danger, abortion is never the answer. In God's eyes, the life of the unborn child and mother are equally sacred. To do evil "so that good may come" is to take God's sovereignty and wisdom into one's own hands (Rom. 3:5–8). In agonizing situations like this, a couple should turn to the prayer of their church:

> Is anyone among you in trouble? Let them pray. Is anyone happy? Let them sing songs of praise. Is anyone among you sick? Let them call the elders of the church to pray over them and anoint them with oil in the name of the Lord. And the prayer offered in faith will make the sick person well; the Lord will raise them up. If they have sinned, they will be forgiven (James 5:13–15).

There is great power and protection in the prayer of a
united church and in the faith that God's will can be done
for both the life of a mother and her unborn child. In the
end – and I say this with trembling – that is what matters.

We must offer alternatives, not moral condemnation.

As Christians, we cannot merely demand an end to abortion without offering a positive alternative. Eberhard
Arnold writes:

> Moral philosophers may demand that the sexual life
> is purified by insisting on purity before and during
> marriage. But even the best of them become insincere
> and unjust if they do not make clear the actual basis for
> the fulfillment of such high demands. Even destruction
> of the life that is waiting to come into being . . . remains
> unassailable without faith in the kingdom of God. The
> supposedly high culture of our days will continue to
> practice this massacre as long as social disorder and
> injustice prevail. Infant murder cannot be overcome as
> long as private life and public life are allowed to main-
> tain their status quo.
>
> Whoever fights against self-centered acquisitiveness
> and against the deceit in unjust social distinctions must
> fight them in a realistic way – a way that demonstrates a
> different way of life as a possibility that actually exists.
> If this is not done, purity in marriage and an end of
> murder cannot be demanded either. Not even for fami-
> lies with the soundest morals can anyone wish the
> blessing of many children, corresponding to the creative
> powers of God's nature.[39]

Here the church has failed miserably. There are so many
teenage mothers who are confronted by this question

daily, yet receive no inner guidance, no emotional or economic support. Many feel they have no other choice than abortion: they have been the victim of sexual abuse; or they fear an angry boyfriend; or their parents have pressured them, saying that if they have the baby they can't come home.

In speaking with groups of women who have had abortions, author Frederica Mathewes-Green discovered a near unanimous consensus as to why women have abortions: in nearly every case it is because of relationships. Women do not want abortions, she writes. They want support and hope.

> I have found that a woman is most likely to choose abortion in order to please or protect the people that she cares about. Often she discovers too late that there is another person to whom she has obligations: her own unborn child. The grief that follows abortion springs from the conviction that, in a crisis, this relationship was fatally betrayed.
>
> Supporting women with unplanned pregnancies means continuing what pregnancy-care centers have been doing all along: providing housing, medical care, clothing, counseling, and so forth. But we should also be paying attention to becoming a steadfast friend, the most important help we can give, and to doing whatever we can to repair relationships in the family circle.[40]

In speaking out against abortion, therefore, we must not forget that few other sins cause more heartache or anguish of soul. Very few women today are offered viable alternatives, and almost none of them are pointed to God, who alone can answer their need. A woman who has had an abortion suffers great torment of conscience, and her isolation and endless pain can be healed only at the cross – only by finding Christ. Christians need to feel the immeasurable pain that so many women bear in their hearts for their lost children. Who of us can cast the first stone? (John 8:7) Woe to us if we ever become cold toward a woman who has had an abortion!

God loves every mother and every unborn child in a very special way. After all, he sent us his only son, Jesus, to earth in the form of a baby, through the womb of a mother. As Mother Teresa points out, even if a mother turns against her unborn child, God will not forget that little soul. He has carved each baby in the palm of his hand and has a plan for each life, not only on earth but for eternity. To those who are desperate enough to hinder God's plan, we say with Mother Teresa, "Please don't kill the child. I want the child. Please give the baby to me."

18

Divorce and Remarriage

*Anyone who divorces his wife and marries another
woman commits adultery, and the man who marries a divorced woman commits adultery.*
Luke 16:18

THE QUESTION of divorce and remarriage is one of
the toughest issues that faces the Christian church in our
time. It is harder and harder to find couples who affirm
the words, "What God has joined together, let no one
put asunder" – couples who believe that marriage means
faithfulness between one man and one woman until
death parts them (Matt. 19:6).

*A marriage bond may break,
but it can never be dissolved.*

The majority of Christians today believe that divorce
and remarriage are morally and biblically permissible.
They argue that though God hates divorce, he allows it
as a concession to our sinful condition. Because of our
hardness of heart, they explain, marriages can "die" or
dissolve. In other words, God recognizes our frailty and
accepts the fact that in a fallen world the ideal cannot
always be realized. Through God's forgiveness, one can
always start again, even if in a new marriage.

But what about the bond that is promised between two
and made – whether knowingly or unknowingly – before
God? Does God's forgiveness ever mean we can deny
it? Does he ever allow unfaithfulness? Just as the unity
of the church is eternal and unchangeable, so true marriage reflects this unity and is indissoluble. Like the early
Christians, I believe that as long as both spouses are living,
there can be no remarriage after divorce. What God has
joined together in the unity of the Spirit is joined together
until death parts a couple. Unfaithfulness, whether by
one or by both partners, cannot change this. No Christian has the freedom to marry someone else as long as his
or her spouse is still living. The bond of unity is at stake.

Jesus is clear that it was because of hard-heartedness that Moses, under the law, allowed divorce (Matt.
19:8). However, among his disciples – those born of the
Spirit – hard-heartedness is no longer a valid excuse.
Moses said, "Anyone who divorces his wife must give
her a certificate of divorce." But Jesus said, "Anyone who
divorces his wife, except for sexual immorality, makes
her the victim of adultery, and anyone who marries a
divorced woman commits adultery" (Matt. 5:31–32). The
disciples understood this decisive word of Jesus clearly:
"If this is the situation between a husband and wife, it is
better not to marry" (Matt. 19:10). Moses gave allowance
to divorce out of sheer necessity, but this hardly changes
the fact that from the beginning marriage was meant to
be indissoluble. A marriage cannot be dissolved (even if
it is broken), neither by the husband who abandons his
adulterous wife, nor by the wife who abandons her adulterous husband. God's order cannot be abolished that
easily or lightly.[41]

Paul writes with the same clarity to the Corinthians:

To the married I give this command (not I, but the Lord): A wife must not separate from her husband. But if she does, she must remain unmarried or else be reconciled to her husband. And a husband must not divorce his wife (1 Cor. 7:10–11).

He also writes, "A woman is bound to her husband as long as he lives. But if her husband dies, she is free to marry anyone she wishes, but he must belong to the Lord" (1 Cor. 7:39). And in Romans he says, "So then, if she has sexual relations with another man while her husband is still alive, she is called an adulteress. But if her husband dies, she is released from that law and is not an adulteress if she marries another man" (Rom. 7:3).

Because adultery is a betrayal of the mysterious union between one man and one woman who become one flesh, it is one of the worst forms of deceit. Adultery must always be squarely confronted by the church, and the adulterer must be called to repentance and disciplined (1 Cor. 5:1–5).

The answer to a broken bond is faithfulness and love.

Even if Jesus allows divorce for reasons of sexual immorality or adultery, it should never be the inevitable result or an excuse to remarry. Jesus' love reconciles and forgives. Those who seek a divorce will always be left with the stain of bitterness on their conscience. No matter how much emotional pain an unfaithful spouse causes, the wounded partner must be willing to forgive. Only when we forgive can we ever hope to receive the forgiveness of God for ourselves (Matt. 6:14–15). Faithful love, to our spouse but especially to Christ, is the only answer to a broken bond.

Kent and Amy, who minister together in the same church in Colorado, were once divorced from each other. Their situation was as desperate as a marriage could get. Yet because they kept the door open to Christ they found each other again. Kent shares:

> From day one, our marriage had gigantic problems, and we began a three-year downward spiral into utter confusion. I thought marriage was just a matter of hanging out with my wife and doing fun things together. I had no idea what hard work it involved. Eventually I became a shell of a person and even despised life at times. I tried doing all the "spiritual" things I was supposed to do: reading the Bible, praying, and talking with others. But it all seemed so futile. Amy and I came from completely opposite backgrounds and, hard as we tried, we couldn't communicate.
>
> The pain grew so great that we decided to separate and to begin divorce proceedings. This was absolutely against my church upbringing, but I felt hopelessly trapped and had to get out. Yet even after we decided to divorce, the pain remained constant. I became so emotionally drained that there were mornings when I couldn't even button my shirt. Unable to cope, I stepped down from my pastoral position. All during this time Amy was utterly devastated. I knew she wanted things to be different, but it was all too overwhelming for me. Despite our commitments to Christ and to each other, we were both completely lost.
>
> To deal with my pain, I resorted to work. I knew that I would get into big time trouble if I allowed myself to become idle or to become involved in another

relationship. So I worked and worked – and worked. Subconsciously I think both Amy and I tried to trust God, but daily I swore to myself that I would never get back together with her. Every time we tried to talk things out, we ended up fighting. It was hopeless.

I came to a point where I couldn't even turn to God anymore. Everything became so pointless, so dead: What did it all matter? Why was I working so hard anyway? Who was I trying to fool? Why try to do God's will if nothing good ever came from it?

But late one night, as I left work, the moon and the stars caught my eye. Something grabbed my heart, and I felt anew God's majesty and mercy. In a matter of seconds I was reduced to tears. In all my pain and despair I began to feel, perhaps for the first time, both my true need and God's unconditional love. Although I had become unfaithful to my promises to God and to my wife, God assured me that he was still faithful to me and that he had not given up on me. That night was a real turning point. By the miracle of God's grace, something inside me began to change.

I wish I could say that there were a lot of miraculous events that brought Amy and me back together again. But there weren't. We found each other through a lot of hard work. There was no instant reunion; it took two years. We had to do a lot of talking and a lot of forgiving. But as we shared, a lot of the pain and the emotion that was there before disappeared. In the end, it was God who rescued us. It was he who helped us keep the door open to him and to each other – in spite of ourselves. It was he who spared us the lie that one's problems are best solved by getting involved with some other, more suitable person.

Our marriage still goes through rough patches. Perhaps it always will. We are still very different from each other. And if I dwell too much on my weaknesses or Amy's, it is tempting to try and find a way out. But God's faithfulness binds us together and preserves our love for each other. And it is this faithfulness that keeps me focused and committed.

Of course, not every marital struggle ends as happily as Kent and Amy's. In my church it has happened several times that a husband or wife leaves the church, becomes unfaithful, divorces his or her spouse, and remarries. Almost every time, the one left behind has decided to remain in our church, faithful to Christ and to his or her marriage vows. Though this is naturally a painful choice – and doubly so when there are children involved – it is part of the cost of discipleship. If we turn to God, he will give us the strength to hold fast.

When I marry a couple, I always ask them the following question, which was formulated by my grandfather, a dissident pastor in Nazi Germany:

My brother, will you never follow your wife – and my sister, will you never follow your husband – in what is wrong? If one of you should turn away from the way of Jesus and want to forsake his church, will you always place faith in our master, Jesus of Nazareth, and unity in his Holy Spirit above your marriage, also when confronted by government authorities? I ask you this in the knowledge that a marriage is built on sand unless it is built on the rock of faith, faith in Jesus, the Christ.

As pertinent today as in its original context, there is deep wisdom in this question. In a sense, it is simply a reminder of the choice set before each of us who claim to be disciples: are we ready to follow Jesus at all costs? Didn't he himself warn us, "If anyone comes to me and does not hate father and mother, wife and children, brothers and sisters – yes, even their own life – such a person cannot be my disciple" (Luke 14:26)?

If a couple takes this warning seriously, it may bring about separation, but the sanctity of their marriage covenant will actually be protected. The issue here is not only marriage as such, but the deeper bond of unity between two people united in Christ and his Holy Spirit (1 Cor. 7:15–16). Whenever a man or woman remains loyal to his or her spouse – no matter how unfaithful that partner may be – it is a witness to this unity. The eternal faithfulness of God and his church can always engender new commitment and hope. I have seen more than once how the faithfulness of a believing partner can lead an unbelieving spouse back to Jesus, back to the church, and back to a strong marriage.

Ann and her husband, Howard (whose story I shared in chapter 16), are an example of this. Even when Howard fell back into sin, Ann never wavered from her commitment to Christ and the church. Yet though she refused to go along with Howard's deceit, she did not judge him. Instead, she quietly led him in the struggle for repentance and a fresh start. Largely as a result of Ann's steadfastness, both their marriage and Howard's faith were restored.

True faithfulness is not merely the absence of adultery.
Though God hates divorce, he will also judge every unloving or dead marriage, and this should be a warning

to each of us. How many of us have been cold-hearted or loveless to our spouses at one time or another? How many thousands of couples, rather than loving each other, merely coexist? True faithfulness is not simply the absence of adultery. It must be a commitment of heart and soul. Whenever husband and wife lack commitment to each other, live parallel lives, or become estranged, separation and divorce lurk around the corner.

It is the task of every church to fight the spirit of adultery wherever it raises its head. Here I am not only speaking of adultery as a physical act; in a sense, anything inside a marriage that weakens love, unity, and purity, or hinders the spirit of mutual reverence, is adultery, because it feeds the spirit of adultery. That is why God speaks of the unfaithfulness of the people of Israel as adultery (Mal. 2:10–16).

In the Old Testament, the prophets use faithfulness in marriage as a picture of God's commitment to Israel, his chosen people – his bride (Hos. 3:1). In a similar way, the Apostle Paul compares marriage to the relationship of unity between Christ, the bridegroom, and his church, the bride. Only in the spirit of these biblical images can we clearly consider the question of divorce and remarriage.

When a church fails to nurture the marriages of its own members, how can it claim innocence when these marriages fall apart? When it shies away from testifying that "what God has joined together, no one should put asunder," how can it expect its married members to remain committed for life?

In considering these questions, there are two pitfalls we must avoid. First, we can never agree to divorce; second, we must never treat those who suffer its need and pain with legalism or rigidity. In rejecting divorce, we cannot reject the divorced person, even if remarried. We must always remember that though Jesus speaks very sharply against sin, he never lacks compassion. But because he longs to redeem and heal every sinner, he requires repentance for every sin. This is also true for every broken marriage.

Clearly, we must never judge. At the same time, however, we must be faithful to Christ above everything else. We must embrace his whole truth – not just those parts of it that seem to fit our needs (Matt. 23:23–24). That is why my church will not marry divorced members (at least as long as a former spouse is still living) and why we cannot accept divorced and remarried couples as members, as long as they continue to live together as husband and wife. Remarriage compounds the sin of divorce and precludes the possibility of reconciliation with one's first spouse. We stand for lifelong fidelity in marriage. No other stand is consistent with real love and truthfulness.

The significance of the marriage commitment needs to be rediscovered. We are only beginning to confront the harm that divorce does to our children. For children, let alone for adults, divorce is something you don't just "get over." Study after study shows that the majority of children whose parents divorce are worried, underachieving, and self-deprecating. Even ten years after their parents break up, they still suffer from such emotional problems as fear and depression, and display antisocial behavior.

Stepfamilies do not provide the answer. The original family structure cannot be restored, however hard one tries to simulate it. In fact, children living with stepparents often show more insecurity than children in single-parent homes.[42] A generation of children is growing up without parents who act as true role models – and many children do not have real parents at all. As well-intentioned as many of today's young people are, where can they find support when it is time to marry and start a family?

With God, all things are possible.

Naturally, if divorce is to be avoided, the church must offer its members guidance and practical support long before their marriages collapse (Heb. 10:24; 12:15). As soon as there are indications that a marriage is at risk, it is best to be honest and open about it. Once a couple drifts too far apart, it may take space as well as time for them to find each other's hearts again. In a situation like this, as in one where a spouse has become abusive, temporary separation may be necessary. Especially when this is the case, the church must find concrete ways to help both spouses – first in seeking repentance and then in finding the mutual trust and forgiveness necessary to restore the marriage.

It is sad that in today's society, faithfulness is so rare that it has come to be seen as a "heroic" virtue. Shouldn't it be taken for granted as the bedrock of our faith? (Gal. 5:22) As followers of Christ, shouldn't each of us be willing to hold firm through thick and thin until death, to Christ, to his church, and to our husband or wife? Only with this resolve can we hope to remain faithful to our marriage vows.

The way of discipleship is a narrow way, but through the cross anyone who hears the words of Jesus can put them into practice (Matt. 7:24). If Jesus' teaching on divorce and remarriage is hard, it is only because so many in our day no longer believe in the power of repentance and forgiveness. It is because we no longer believe that what God joins together can, by his grace, be held together; and that, as Jesus says, "With God, all things are possible."

Nothing should be too hard for us when it is a requirement of the gospel (Matt. 11:28–30). If we look at Jesus' teaching on divorce and remarriage in this faith, we will see that it is one of great promise, hope, and strength. It is a teaching whose righteousness is much greater than that of the moralists and philosophers. It is the righteousness of the kingdom, and it is based on the reality of resurrection and new life.

19

Therefore
Let Us Keep Watch

*The night is nearly over; the day is almost here. So
let us put aside the deeds of darkness and put on
the armor of light. Let us behave decently, as in the
daytime, not in carousing and drunkenness, not in
sexual immorality and debauchery, not in dissension and jealousy. Rather, clothe yourselves with
the Lord Jesus Christ, and do not think about how
to gratify the desires of the flesh.*

Romans 13:12–14

DESPITE THE SHAMELESSNESS and promiscuity
of our time, purity and faithful love are still possible
today. Even if many churches have neglected to proclaim
the message that sexual happiness is possible within the
commitment of marriage alone, we can still be certain
of its truth. There is no question that many people today
have a deep longing for purity and faithfulness. But
longing is not enough. Only when we are willing to follow
and obey the leading of the Holy Spirit, cost what it may,
can we experience its great blessings in our daily lives. Do
we believe deeply enough in the power of the Spirit? Are
we willing to let God transform our hearts so completely
that he turns our lives upside down? (Rom. 12:2)

The struggle for purity demands daily resolve.

All of us know temptation, and all of us have given in to temptation. We have all failed at one time or another – in our relationships at work and at home, in our marriages, and in our personal lives. The sooner we face that, the better. Yet we can take comfort, even if we struggle with ups and downs, and even if our moments of victory are followed by moments of doubt. Even Jesus was tempted, and he was tempted in every way we are (Heb. 4:15). With his help we can find the purity that protects us from every temptation. James says, "Blessed is anyone who endures temptation" (James 1:12 NRSV). What matters here is the deepest will of our heart – the will that speaks within us whenever we come before God in prayer.

As we struggle to be faithful, it is of greatest importance that our entire will is decided for purity. A divided heart will never be able to stand (James 1:6–7). But will-power alone cannot bring about single-mindedness. If we work ourselves into an inner frenzy, even if we manage to keep our head above water, we will soon tire out and sink. Only if we surrender to Jesus can the power of his grace fill us and give us new strength and resolve.

In combating the spirit of our age, we must fight not only against the obvious sins of sexual immorality, deceit, murder, and so on, but also against apathy and fear. Hardly anyone will say that he is against faithfulness and love, or opposed to justice and peace, but how many of us are ready to fight for these things in word and in deed? The spirit of our time has dulled us with such a deathly complacency that we are usually content to look the other way. But if we do not speak out against the evil of our time through the actions of our lives, then we are just as guilty as those who sin deliberately. We must all change, and we must start by confronting the indifference in our own lives.

A little over half a century ago, most people recognized extramarital sex, divorce, homosexual activity, and the like as morally wrong. But today these things are regarded as acceptable lifestyle alternatives. Sadly, an increasing number of churches take this stance as well. Now bestiality (sex with animals), polygamy and polyamorous relationships, and sadomasochism are gaining support as means of "sexual expression." Only a few decades ago, transsexualism – the practice of undergoing a surgical male-to-female or female-to-male sex change – was unheard of. Today this godless practice has become widely accepted in the western world. The enormous cost of these surgeries alone is a crime against humanity when one thinks of the widespread hunger and poverty in the underdeveloped world and even in our own cities.

Frightening as all these trends are, parents should not be afraid to warn their children about the horror of these perversions. For even though Jesus says that all sin can be forgiven, my experience in counseling has shown me that those who engage in such practices can permanently wound their souls.

What must God think of the shamelessness of our time? In *The Brothers Karamazov*, Dostoevsky reminds us that "if God does not exist, everything is permissible." Are we not now seeing "everything?" When will we stop to consider the horrifying spirit of rebellion behind our sinfulness, and remember God's warnings about his wrath on sinners in the end time? Let us remember the words of Paul: "A man reaps what he sows" (Gal. 6:7). Let us ask God for the mercy of his judgment before it is too late. Let us ask him to shake our deadened consciences, to cleanse us, and to bring us new life.

We desperately need more people like John the Baptist today. But where are they? Where are the "voices in the wilderness" crying out for repentance, conversion, faith, and a new life? John's message was simple: "Repent, for the kingdom of God is at hand!" He was not afraid to confront anyone, including the leaders of his day. He even confronted King Herod on his adulterous marriage, saying, "It is not lawful for you to have her" (Matt. 14:3–4). Perhaps most significant, though, he called to account the devout and religious, the "good" people: "You brood of vipers! Who warned you to flee from the coming wrath? Produce fruit in keeping with repentance" (Matt. 3:7–8).

> *In the fight for God's kingdom, good deeds*
> *are not enough.*

In the Gospel of Matthew, Jesus says to his disciples, "The harvest is plentiful but the workers are few" (Matt. 9:37). How much truer is this today! So many people long for the freedom of Christ but remain chained to their sins. So few people dare to stick out their necks. The task is great.

Most of us have good intentions; we earnestly desire to do good deeds and to live rightly. But that is not enough. We dare not forget that the battle for God's kingdom is not just against human nature: we are dealing with something far more powerful, with powers and principalities

(Eph. 6:12), and with the destructive, demonic spirit that John calls the "beast from the abyss" (Rev. 11:7).

This beast holds sway over every country and every government, and its mark is to be found everywhere in our day: in the disappearance of lasting friendship and community, in the oppression of the poor, and in the exploitation of women and children. It is to be seen in the wholesale murder of the unborn and the execution of the imprisoned. Most of all, it is to be seen in the lonely desperation of so many millions of people.

We are living in the end time. It is the last hour (1 John 2:18). We must be on the watch continually if we are not to fall under judgment in the last hour of temptation. We need to seek the inner strength and courage to speak up for God and his cause, even if no one seems willing to hear us.

Jesus' parable of the ten virgins should be a warning and a challenge to all of us. Jesus is not speaking here about the lost world on the one hand and the church on the other: all ten of the women in the story are virgins, and all of them are preparing to meet him. He is challenging the church:

> At that time the kingdom of heaven will be like ten virgins who took their lamps and went out to meet the bridegroom. Five of them were foolish and five were wise. The foolish ones took their lamps but did not take any oil with them. The wise ones, however, took oil in jars along with their lamps. The bridegroom was a long time in coming, and they all became drowsy and fell asleep.
>
> At midnight the cry rang out: "Here's the bridegroom! Come out to meet him!"

Then all the virgins woke up and trimmed their lamps. The foolish ones said to the wise, "Give us some of your oil; our lamps are going out."

"No," they replied, "there may not be enough for both us and you. Instead, go to those who sell oil and buy some for yourselves."

But while they were on their way to buy the oil, the bridegroom arrived. The virgins who were ready went in with him to the wedding banquet. And the door was shut.

Later the others also came. "Lord, Lord," they said, "open the door for us!"

But he replied, "Truly I tell you, I don't know you."

Therefore keep watch, because you do not know the day or the hour (Matt. 25:1–13).

Are we willing to demonstrate that a new way exists?

We cannot merely run from the challenge of sin. Instead, we must live in active protest against everything that opposes God. We must openly fight everything that cheapens or destroys life, everything that leads to separation and division. But we must also recognize that protest alone, which often leads to violence, is not sufficient. To simply renounce the world, reject marriage, or refuse all pleasure would be fruitless.

We must demonstrate that a new way exists and show the world a new reality, the reality of God's righteousness and holiness, which is opposed to the spirit of this world. We must show with our lives that men and women can live lives of purity, peace, unity, and love wherever they dedicate their energies to working for the common good; and not only by creating spiritual community, but by building up a practical life of sharing. Above all, we must witness to the power of love. Each of us can give our lives to others in the service of love. That is God's will for humankind (John 13:34–35).

In order to demonstrate God's will, the church must first take concrete steps toward forming a genuine sexual counterculture. This demands committed effort. Chastity programs are not enough. Marriages and families will continue to splinter unless the church forms a life together on totally different terms. Christian families, along with their ministers, need to pledge to live their personal and social lives in contrast to the ways of the world. Unless we relate to each other on a different plane from the world's, we have little to protest or to say. If we are going to be serious about pursuing purity in this world, then we will need to hold each other, as brothers and sisters, accountable. This applies to everyday life: the way we dress and look, what we allow into our homes, how we and our children relate to the opposite sex.

The visible witness of such a community will do far more to convince our society than a million pamphlets on abstinence. Christian ideals can be explained, but moral principles are never enough. Only when the world sees living proof that a Christ-centered sexual life is possible – one where true freedom goes hand in hand with reverence and responsibility – will people welcome such values and norms.

However, wherever God's will is consistently lived out, it will be misunderstood and seen as provocation (1 Pet. 4:4). Two thousand years have not made our present world any more tolerant of Jesus' message than the world of his time. Those who are unwilling to accept his way will always be resentful and even vindictive toward those who witness to it, and a clash is inevitable (John 15:18–20). But if we who claim to follow Christ are afraid to live out his commands because we fear persecution, who will do it? And if it is not the task of the church to bring the darkness of the world into the light of Christ, whose is it?

Our hope is in God's coming kingdom, which is the wedding feast of the Lamb. Let us wait faithfully for that day. Every word we say, everything we do, should be inspired and influenced by our expectation. Every relationship, every marriage, should be a symbol of it. Jesus, the bridegroom, expects a bride prepared and waiting for him. But when he comes, will we be ready? Will we be "a radiant church, without stain or wrinkle"? (Eph. 5:27) Or will we be full of excuses? (Luke 14:15–24)

We must never be afraid of the ridicule and slander our witness will bring on us. What grips us and drives us should be God's future – the wonderful future of his kingdom – not the present "realities" of human society. It is God who holds the final hour of history in his hands, and each day of our lives should be a preparation for that hour.

A Call to Purity

A Joint Statement of the
Roman Catholic Archdiocese of New York
and the Bruderhof Communities

September 22, 2014

THE ROMAN CATHOLIC ARCHDIOCESE of New York and the Bruderhof communities believe that God has intervened in human history – decisively – in the birth of his only son Jesus Christ, in his life, teaching, crucifixion, and resurrection. Jesus teaches that "I am the way, and the truth, and the life; no one comes to the Father, but by me" (John 14:6). It is the person of Jesus Christ, Son of God, who has revealed to us the fullness of God's truth and love.

God created every one of us to exist for him and for others. "You shall love the Lord your God with all your heart, and with all your soul, and with all your mind, and with all your strength," and "you shall love your neighbor as yourself. There is no other commandment greater than these" (Mark 12:30–31). We are born to love purely. Purity between people – between man and woman in marriage, and between all persons in the single life – is God's will and brings joy. Purity requires faithfulness and readiness for self-sacrifice: "If anyone would be my follower, he must deny his very self, take up his cross daily, and follow me. For whoever would save his life will lose it; and whoever loses his life for my sake will save it" (Luke 9:23–24).

Concerning marriage, Pope John Paul II wrote in his Apostolic Letter on the Dignity and Vocation of Women: "Man and woman are called from the beginning not only to exist 'side by side' or 'together,' but they are also called to exist mutually 'one for the other'. . . . On the basis of the principle of mutuality being 'for' the other in interpersonal 'communion,' there develops in humanity itself, in accordance with God's will, the integration of what is 'masculine' and 'feminine'" (*Mulieris Dignitatem*, no. 7).

In the same spirit, the Bruderhof communities' *Foundations of Our Faith and Calling* states: "Christ declared marriage to be the lifelong union of one man and one woman joined together by God, holy and instituted by him from the beginning: 'From the beginning of creation, God made them male and female. For this reason a man shall leave his father and his mother and be joined to his wife, and the two shall become one flesh. Therefore what God has joined together, let no one separate' (Mark 10:6–9). . . . As a creation of God, marriage is not a human invention. It is a sacrament that precedes and transcends the authority of the state. When a man and a woman become one flesh in marriage, their union has a deep connection with God. He made man and woman for each other, each in his image and likeness, and yet each incomplete without the other. He intended their union – a relationship unlike any other – for the bearing and rearing of children" (*Foundations*, nos. 77–78).

We believe that human sexuality is a marvelous gift from God, given to all but intended to be expressed in the sexual act only in the marriage of a man and a woman, and otherwise in chaste friendship. It is clear, however, that over the last half-century human sexuality and purity have been undermined greatly in our culture. Human sin will always lead us to fall short of embracing God's plan completely.

But in western culture especially, lust is being given freer reign. Lust is too often stimulated and exploited for material profit in much of the mass media. Sins of adultery, pornography, premarital sexual intercourse, masturbation, contraception, homosexual practice, and divorce and remarriage have become increasingly accepted, even by those who say they are faithful to Jesus Christ. These practices are openly championed and are often protected by civil law. One result of this is a weakening of faithfulness in marriage and a loss of the sense of the sacredness of the marriage covenant.

The vision of life communicated to us through Jesus Christ gives us the confidence and power to confront these problems. The gospel is Good News! We proclaim the gospel of life, the good news of life: "I came that they might have life, and have it abundantly" (John 10:10).

Jesus knows our temptations and gives us direction, strength, and grace to overcome them. In Christian marriage, the unity of husband and wife reflect the unity of Christ and his Church. Their mutual marriage vows are made in the presence of Christ and his Church. Marriage is sacred, and it is indissoluble. Marriage has the blessing of God and the Church, and that blessing is experienced by the married couple as mutual service, purity, beauty, and joy. Marriage is both unitive and procreative. The two become one flesh in the sight of God. With profound reverence, husband and wife know that in this act of supreme love and self-giving they open themselves to becoming co-creators with God to bring new life into the world. Each child born to them is a blessed gift as well as a new responsibility. Through the love of their father and mother, children get their first sense of the love of God.

Any form of sexual self-gratification is an affront to the purity of marriage, and with God's help must be overcome.

Sexual impurity infects and weakens the marriage relationship whenever one of the couple or both use the other
as a sex object. Paul gives a clear guide for the Christian
and married life: "The fruit of the Spirit is love, joy, peace,
patience, kindness, goodness, faithfulness, gentleness,
and self-control" (Galatians 5:22–23).

A very special gift is given to every man or woman who
is called to a life of celibacy in the service of God and his
or her fellow human beings. When circumstances, rather
than choice, lead to a single life, there is a special challenge to witness to purity and service. Men and women in
that position need both the grace of God and the understanding and support of all Christians.

Out of love for Christ and for all people, it is impera-
tive that leaders of the Christian community encourage
believing Christians to stand and affirm the virtue of
purity. It is in this spirit that the Roman Catholic Archdiocese of New York and the Bruderhof communities
are working together. As brothers and sisters in Christ,
we embrace each other with respect and shared love and
a common concern for a society that has been darkened
by the consequences of sin. Despite the fact that certain
doctrinal differences exist, our two faith communities
stand together in the name of the gospel to make a joint
plea to all people of good will to embrace the power of
purity, decency, and virtuous living in their sexuality.

According to the *Catechism of the Catholic Church,*
purity, modesty, and God's grace are integral to the Christian life. In a section entitled "The Battle for Purity," the
Church declares: "Purity requires modesty, an integral
part of temperance. . . . Modesty protects the mystery
of persons and their love. It encourages patience and
moderation in loving relationships; it requires that the
conditions for the definitive giving and commitment of

man and woman to one another be fulfilled. . . . Christian purity requires a purification of the social climate. It requires of the communications media that their presentations show concern for respect and restraint. . . . So-called moral permissiveness rests on an erroneous conception of human freedom; the necessary precondition for the development of true freedom is to let oneself be educated in the moral law. . . . The Good News of Christ continually renews the life and culture of fallen man; it combats and removes error and evil, which flow from the ever-present attraction of sin. It never ceases to purify and elevate the morality of peoples. It takes the spiritual qualities and endowments of every age and nation, and with supernatural riches it causes them to blossom, as it were from within; it fortifies, completes, and restores them in Christ" (CCC, nos. 2520–2527).

In his book *Sex, God, and Marriage,* Bruderhof senior pastor Johann Christoph Arnold calls upon all people to embrace a pure life. "Too many people today have simply given up on the possibility of a pure life. They have bought into the myth of sexual 'liberation' and tried to live with its disappointments, and when their relationships fall apart, they explain away their failures. They fail to see what a tremendous gift purity is. . . . Wherever there is a faithful church – a community of people who are committed to living in genuine and honest relationships – there is help and hope for every person and every marriage" (*Sex, God, and Marriage,* fifth edition, pages xvi–xvii).

Our common calling to follow Christ and our shared desire to encourage people of goodwill to live a life of purity bring together our two communities of faith. The Roman Catholic Archdiocese of New York and the Bruderhof communities exhort all people – especially those baptized in the name of Christ – to live a chaste life. Seeking the power of God's grace, both communities plead for purity. There is no greater need in our culture today, and for every human heart, than to know God's love and to embrace it in living our fundamental call to holiness of life. This is especially true for our children, who need our example so they may learn to embrace the way of Jesus Christ as their only path to happiness and fulfillment in life.

It is our hope and prayer that people everywhere will open their hearts to the transforming power of true love. And we recognize that if we lack courage to confront and inspire our members with Christ's truth, our efforts on account of morality will have but little effect. A pure mind, body, and soul are essential to a life of happiness and peace. Despite the obstacles placed by weakening moral standards, building a culture of life and love, according to God's plan, is possible. Let us never forget that God wills the best for each human being, and that for him, "all things are possible" (Matt. 19:26). Amen.

Timothy Cardinal Dolan
Archbishop of New York

Johann Christoph Arnold
Senior Pastor, Bruderhof

Notes

1. For a readable summary of current findings on the effects of non-marital sex, read *The Ring Makes All the Difference: The Hidden Consequences of Cohabitation and the Strong Benefits of Marriage,* by Glenn T. Stanton (Chicago: Moody Publishers, 2011).

2. Christoph Friedrich Blumhardt and Johann Christoph Blumhardt, *Now Is Eternity* (Farmington, PA: Plough, 1999), 28. Christoph Friedrich Blumhardt (1842–1919) was a German pastor, author, and religious socialist.

3. Thomas Merton, *New Seeds of Contemplation* (New York: New Directions, 1972), 180.

4. Augustine of Hippo, *Sermons,* 75.7.

5. Friedrich E. F. von Gagern, *Der Mensch als Bild: Beiträge zur Anthropologie,* 2nd ed. (Frankfurt am Main: Verlag Josef Knecht, 1955), 32. Von Gagern (b. 1914) was a German Catholic psychiatrist.

6. Friedrich Nietzsche, *Thus Spake Zarathustra,* trans. R. J. Hollingdale (London: Penguin Books, 1961), 95.

7. *Der Mensch als Bild,* 33–34.

8. Dietrich Bonhoeffer, *Ethics* (New York: Macmillan, 1975), 19.

9. *Der Mensch als Bild,* 58.

10. Eberhard Arnold, *Love and Marriage in the Spirit* (Rifton, NY: Plough, 1965), 152.

11. J. Heinrich Arnold, *Discipleship* (Farmington, PA: Plough, 1994), 42.

12. Eberhard Arnold, *Innerland* (Farmington, PA: Plough, 1999), 37.

13. Dietrich Bonhoeffer, *The Cost of Discipleship* (New York: Macmillan, 1958), 95–96.

14. Cf. John J. Friesen, trsl. and ed., *Peter Riedemann's Hutterite Confession of Faith* (Scottdale, PA: Herald Press, 1999), 127.

15. *Discipleship,* 160–161.

16. Ernst Rolffs, ed., *Tertullian, der Vater des abendländischen Christentums: Ein Kämpfer für und gegen die römische Kirche* (Berlin: Hochweg, 1930), 31–32.

17. Jean Vanier, *Man and Woman He Made Them* (New York: Paulist, 1994), 128.

Notes

18 Friedrich von Gagern, *Man and Woman: An Introduction to the Mystery of Marriage* (Cork, Ireland: Mercier, 1957), 26–27.

19 I explore this theme in great depth in my book *Why Children Matter* (Rifton, NY: Plough, 2012).

20 Johann Christoph Blumhardt and Christoph Friedrich Blumhardt, *Thoughts About Children* (Rifton, NY: Plough, 1980), 29.

21 *Thoughts About Children,* 9.

22 *Discipleship,* 169.

23 *Discipleship,* 177–178.

24 Dietrich Bonhoeffer, *The Martyred Christian: 160 Readings* (New York: Collier Macmillan, 1985), 170.

25 Eberhard Arnold, *The Early Christians: In Their Own Words* (Farmington, PA: Plough, 1997), 15.

26 *The Wall Street Journal,* Dec. 10, 1993.

27 Numerous studies, including those conducted by Planned Parenthood, conclude that teens who have been through a typical sex education course have a much higher rate of sexual activity than those who have not. For more information on teenage sexual activity contact: Center for Parent/ Youth Understanding, www.cpyu.org.

28 "Church report accepts cohabiting couples," *The Tablet,* June 10, 1995.

29 See Andreas J. Kostenberger, *God, Marriage and Family* (Wheaton, IL: Crossway Books, 2004), ch. 10 for an excellent, readable summary of the biblical teaching on homosexuality.

30 Many also argue that since Jesus never spoke out against committed same-sex relationships, they must not be sinful. Not only is this an argument from silence (Jesus also never speaks out against incest), but it ignores the fact that Jesus, as a faithful Jew, simply assumed that marriage was between one man and one woman (Matt. 19:1–10). For a rigorous refutation of common contemporary objections to the biblical teaching against homosexuality, see Robert A. J. Gagnon, *The Bible and Homosexual Practice: Texts and Hermeneutics* (Nashville: Abingdon, 2001).

31 Sherif Girgis, Robert P. George, and Ryan T. Anderson, *What is Marriage? Man and Woman: A Defense* (New York: Encounter Books, 2012).

32 A beautifully written and honest book about what it means to live with same-sex attractions is Wesley Hill's *Washed and Waiting: Reflections on Christian Faithfulness and Homosexuality* (Grand Rapids, MI: Zondervan, 2010).

33 Eberhard Arnold, *God's Revolution* (Farmington, PA: Plough, 1997), 135.

34 I explore this more fully in *Their Name Is Today: Reclaiming Childhood in a Hostile World* (Walden, NY: Plough, 2014).

35 Stanley Hauerwas, *Unleashing the Scripture: Freeing the Bible from Captivity to America* (Nashville: Abingdon, 1993), 131.

36 Mother Teresa, speech at National Prayer Breakfast, Washington DC, February 3, 1994.

37 Michael J. Gorman, *Abortion and the Early Church: Christian, Jewish, and Pagan Attitudes in the Greco-Roman World* (New York: Paulist, 1982), 47–62.

38 *Ethics,* 164.

39 *Innerland,* 116–117.

40 Frederica Mathewes-Green, "Perspective," *The Plough* 56 (Spring 1998), 33.

41 If divorce and remarriage are never justified, then why does Jesus allow marital unfaithfulness as an exception? (Matt. 5:32; 19:9) He may well have said this because Jewish law required a husband to divorce an adulterous wife (e.g. Matt. 1:19). However, he does not say divorce is always required in such a situation, nor does he apply this exception to remarriage.

42 *Why Marriage Matters, Third Edition: Thirty Conclusions from the Social Sciences* (New York: Institute for American Values, 2011).

For Further Reading

Arnold, Eberhard and Emmy von Hollander. *Love Letters*. Rifton, NY: Plough, 2007. More than a collection of love letters, this book shows how a man and a woman can nurture each other in following Christ.

Arnold, Eberhard. *God's Revolution*. Farmington, PA: Plough, 1983. Topically arranged excerpts from the author's talks and writings on community, marriage, the family, children, and the church.

Arnold, Johann Christoph. *Their Name Is Today: Reclaiming Childhood in a Hostile World*. Walden, NY: Plough, 2014. From ordinary educators and parents, real stories of empowerment and hope against all odds.

Arnold, Johann Christoph. *Why Children Matter*. Rifton, NY: Plough, 2012. Practical and down-to-earth advice on raising and educating children.

Arnold, J. Heinrich. *Discipleship*. Farmington, PA: Plough, 1994. Thoughts on following Christ in the daily grind, topically arranged. Includes sections on sex, love, marriage, parenting, and celibacy.

Arnold, J. Heinrich. *Freedom From Sinful Thoughts*. Rifton, NY: Plough, 1997. Spiritual insights on the struggle to overcome personal sins and temptations.

Bloesch, Donald G. *Is the Bible Sexist?* Westchester, IL: Crossway, 1982. A sane and sober approach to the volatile issue of feminism in the church that is both sensitive to women's concerns and solidly grounded in the Bible.

Bonhoeffer, Dietrich. *Life Together*. New York: Harper and Brothers, 1954. A time-honored manifesto on one of the most essential aspects of being: solitude, interaction, and community.

Chesterton, G.K. *Brave New Family*. San Francisco: Ignatius, 1990. Prophetic and insightful essays on love, sex, marriage, gender roles, children, and the institution of the family in western society.

Clapp, Rodney. *Families at the Crossroads*. Downers Grove, IL: InterVarsity, 1993. A thoughtful discussion on the role of the church in family life from a biblical perspective.

Cornes, Andrew. *Divorce and Remarriage*. Grand Rapids, MI: Eerdmans, 1993. One of the most thorough biblical and pastoral treatments of this difficult subject.

Fromm, Erich. *The Art of Loving*. New York: Harper Collins, 1989. Reflections on the definition and meaning of love.

Gagern, Friedrich E. F. von. *Difficulties in Married Life*. New York: Paulist, 1964. Thoughtful advice from an experienced Catholic psychiatrist.

Gagern, Friedrich E. F. von. *Man and Woman: An Introduction to the Mystery of Marriage*. Cork, Ireland: Mercier, 1957. Sex education with an emphasis on reverence as the key to healthy sexuality.

Gagnon, Robert A.J. *The Bible and Homosexual Practice*. Nashville, TN: Abingdon Press, 2001. Perhaps the most scholarly and comprehensive treatment on the biblical teaching regarding homosexuality.

Gorman, Michael J. *Abortion and the Early Church*. New York: Paulist, 1982. A readable and concise treatment on the early church's stand against abortion.

Harris, Joshua. *I Kissed Dating Goodbye*. Colorado Springs, CO: Multnomah Books, 2003. This book shows the pitfalls of the conventional dating game and points young adults toward a lifestyle of purity, in which true friendships can blossom.

Hildebrand, Dietrich von. *Purity: The Mystery of Christian Sexuality*. Steubenville, OH: Franciscan University Press, 1989. A masterful work on the meaning of purity – and Christ's call to a pure life.

Hildebrand, Dietrich von. *Man and Woman: Love and the Meaning of Intimacy*. Manchester, NH: Sophia Institute, 1992. A lucid discussion of the nature of love and the mystery of sexuality.

Hollinger, Dennis P. *The Meaning of Sex: Christian Ethics and the Moral Life.* Grand Rapids, MI: Baker Academic, 2009. A readable but very thorough treatment of sexual ethics from a Christian perspective.

Laney, J. Carl. *The Divorce Myth.* Minneapolis: Bethany House, 1981. A compassionate but uncompromising challenge to the institutions of divorce and remarriage, from a biblical perspective.

Mathewes-Green, Frederica. *Real Choices: Listening to Women; Looking for Alternatives to Abortion.* Felicity Press, 2013. A sensitive look at the real reasons why women choose abortion and how to help them find meaningful alternatives.

Neuer, Werner. *Man and Woman in Christian Perspective.* Wheaton, IL: Crossway, 1991. A biblical discussion of the similarities and differences between men and women.

Stanton, Glenn T. *The Ring Makes all the Difference: The Hidden Consequences of Cohabitation and the Strong Benefits of Marriage.* Chicago: Moody Press, 2011. This book is a highly readable presentation of up-to-date research on the dire consequences of marital breakdown in our society.

Vanier, Jean. *Community and Growth.* New York: Paulist, 1989. A bestselling collection of readings, topically arranged, calling for a radical turn from the disintegration and divisiveness of contemporary society to love, mutual support, and community.

Yarhouse, Mark A. *Homosexuality and the Christian.* Minneapolis: Bethany House Publishers, 2010). An excellent resource to understand and help one who is homosexual.

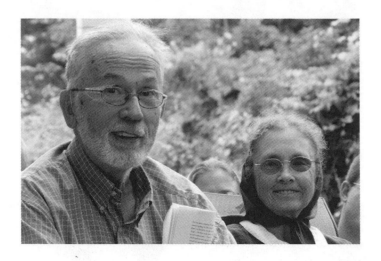

The Author

JOHANN CHRISTOPH ARNOLD is a noted speaker and writer on marriage, parenting, education, and end-of-life issues, and a senior pastor of the Bruderhof, a movement of Christian communities. With his wife, Verena, he has counseled thousands of individuals and families over the last forty years. Over a million copies of his books are in print in more than twenty languages.

Arnold's message has been shaped by encounters with great peacemakers such as Martin Luther King Jr., Mother Teresa, Dorothy Day, César Chavez, and Pope John Paul II. Together with paralyzed police officer Steven McDonald, Arnold started Breaking the Cycle, a program that works with students at hundreds of public high schools to promote reconciliation through forgiveness. He also serves as chaplain for the local sheriff's department.

The author greets Pope Francis and presents a copy of Sex, God, and Marriage *before they address an international, interfaith conference on marriage in November 2014.*

Born in England in 1940 to German refugees, Arnold spent his boyhood years in South America, and immigrated to the United States in 1955. He and his wife have eight children, forty-four grandchildren, and one great-grandchild. They live in upstate New York.